P9-CKY-236

The Truth About The CAJUNS

Trent Angers

Published by:
ACADIAN HOUSE PUBLISHING
Lafayette, Louisiana

ISBN: 0-925417-04-1

Printed in the United States of America

In memory of my father,
ROBERT J. ANGERS JR.,
who walked among the Cajuns all his life
and who treated them, as well as all others,
with the respect and dignity
that he believed their Creator
intended them to have.

ABOUT THE COVER: Many people of French-Acadian, or Cajun, descent have distinguished themselves in various fields of endeavor. Among them are (clockwise, starting with the man at top right): the entrepreneur, Roland Dugas, president and co-founder of Acadian Ambulance Service, one of the largest and most proficient ambulance companies in the nation; the award-winning broadcast journalist, Howard K. Smith, first with CBS and later with ABC News; the famous Cajun chef, Paul Prudhomme, who has done more to bring attention to Cajun food nationwide than anyone alive today; the professional athlete, Bobby Hebert, quarterback for the New Orleans Saints; and the successful businesswoman and former beauty queen, Kathy Hebert Smith, who was Miss Louisiana and third runner-up in the Miss U.S.A. contest. (Photos and more information on these and other accomplished people of Acadian descent can be found starting on page 33.)

—Illustration by Pat Soper, Lafayette, La.

— Contents —

Acknowledgements

Several people gave generously of their time, energy and knowledge to help bring this book to fruition, and I am indebted to them because of it. Glenn Conrad, director of the Center for Louisiana Studies, and Carl Brasseaux, assistant director of the Center, both shared valuable insights about the Cajuns of today and yesterday and read and critiqued some of the chapters. Winston DeVille, one of Louisiana's leading genealogists, my wife, Cindi Angers and my brother, Glenn Angers, all read and critiqued the manuscript. Amy Baltazar, Georgia Green and Melissa Jones provided patient assistance in the research phase.

—T.A.

Preface

When I set out to write this book, I mentioned my plans to a number of acquaintances — teachers, store owners, fellow journalists. The immediate response from seven out of ten of them was identical:

"It's about time someone finally does it."

This encouraged me in my belief that the Cajun people of south Louisiana are being treated shoddily by some of the media — and have been for quite some time.

In talking with these acquaintances, I learned that they were embarrassed and some of them were downright angry over the way the Cajuns were being portrayed in the media nationally. The word "exploited" came up frequently; so did the word "demeaning."

I don't think it's being unduly defensive for one to object to the outlandish manner in which the Cajuns are being described in some of the national and regional magazines. One proclaimed, "Cajuns are nothing if not jolly." Another reported, "In Cajun country...everybody's a cousin and everything's cooked in cayenne by a people whose religion is hospitality, whose devotion to passing a good time, *cher,* is one of this anxious world's purer states of grace...."

The Cajun people have a heritage and culture of which they are justifiably proud. They have managed to retain their ethnic identity and customs more than many groups of Americans.

It is this uniqueness that has attracted reporters from throughout the U.S. and beyond. Some of the stories that have resulted have been well done, thoroughly researched and sensitively written portrayals of a warm, unique group of Americans. But many more have been shallow, stereotyping pieces that have tended to show the Cajuns as people who place an inordinate emphasis upon eating, drinking and dancing.

Seeing and hearing about these stories concerned me both as a citizen of south Louisiana and as a journalist. What has happened to journalism in this country today? Have some travel writers been exempted from the rules of responsibility and accuracy? Are these guys flying in for a day or two, taking in the swamp tour, hanging around a Cajun dance hall for a while, reading a few tourist brochures, and writing a story based on just that?

It's too bad, but some reporters are spending long hours and turning out fine stories except for one or two inaccurate or stereotyping sentences — which have a way of tainting the article and calling its overall credibility into question.

The Cajuns' good name would be taking enough of a beating if these stories were appearing in obscure magazines or tiny-circulation newspapers. But some of the articles have showed up in publications like *Esquire, Gentleman's Quarterly, Town & Country, The Chicago Tribune* and *The Washington Post.*

Not to be outdone by the magazines and newspapers, some of the movies, books and various sorts of "documentaries" floating around the country in recent years have also stereotyped and thus demeaned the Cajuns.

The purpose of this book is to set the record straight on just who the Cajuns really are. It is designed to help dispel the stereotypes and some of the myths about the Cajuns, their food and their environment. It is also to point out that the Cajuns have a very real image problem, one that not only has undermined the dignity of the people, but also scared off some of the potential new industry that is sorely needed in Louisiana today. This image problem is analyzed in later chapters and some solutions to the problem are offered.

In refuting the articles that depict the Cajuns as being hedonists constantly in pursuit of good times, I don't want to go overboard in the opposite direction by creating an image of boring, humorless, stick-in-the-mud types who have no joy in their lives. Because that surely isn't the case. So, included is a chapter on Cajun humor, with a sampling of the jokes that are going around south Louisiana these days. Many people in this area are offended by the jokes of the old Cajun humorists that tend to portray the Cajuns as dull-witted. But there is a whole new breed of humorist stepping forward these days, and their stuff seems to be catching on. An appreciation of good humor is one of the aspects of the *joie de vivre* (joy of life) that so many visitors say they see in the people of the Cajun country.

Another thing visitors observe is that Cajun food is better

than the average American fare, much better. So, included is a chapter that explains what Cajun food is and offers several sample recipes. Traditional Cajun food is not peppery hot, despite what some magazines are saying and what some restaurants are serving nowadays.

I've been living in the Cajun country for 40 years, and I've been working as a journalist here for more than 20. From this vantage point, I submit that the Cajuns have not been portrayed in the national media with the accuracy and the dignity to which they are entitled.

To depict them as somewhat simple-minded and unduly concerned with eating, drinking and dancing just isn't accurate — or fair. But, to say generally that they seem to have the ability to enjoy life and that they are strongly family-oriented, as well as industrious and good-hearted, this would be closer to the truth.

—TRENT ANGERS

The Truth About The CAJUNS

Chapter One

You Just Can't Believe Everything You Read About The Cajuns These Days

EVER SINCE HENRY Wadsworth Longfellow wrote the poem, "Evangeline," back in the 1800s, writers have had a tendency to play it fast and loose with the facts about the French-Acadian people, known today as Cajuns.

Longfellow's poem is rooted in the factual history of the Acadian exile, which began in 1755. He spices up his story and brings it to life by creating two fictitious characters, Evangeline and Gabriel, an engaged couple who are separated during the exile from Nova Scotia and reunited only when Gabriel is on his death bed many years later. It's a nice story, but it's not true. It is a fictional piece based on a factual event in history.

Similarly, some of the stories about the Cajuns in the media today are so dramatic, so romanticized that they, too, seem almost like fiction.

You see, the American media rediscovered the Cajun country for the second or third time this century around 1982. And since then, tourism here has picked up greatly, Cajun food has become known all over the country, and seemingly everyone who has worked for a national magazine or newspaper this decade has showed up in south Louisiana to do a story.

While some of these stories are thorough and accurate, others are seriously flawed, to put it mildly. Many of the articles about the Cajuns and their land can only be described as superficial, distorted works done by writers who were either short on time, short on competence, or so burdened down with preconceived notions that a well-balanced story was virtually impossible to begin with.

To read some of these stories, you'd swear that all the Cajuns do is eat, drink and dance! They are portrayed as a glib bunch of beer-drinkin', two-steppin', party-goin' types who are a bit short on intelligence, integrity and ingenuity.

It's true that the Cajun people and their culture are noticeably different than mainstream America in some ways. But these differences have been exaggerated to the point that some of the stories border on fiction.

Rather than taking the time and making the effort to portray them accurately, too many writers have described the Cajuns in stereotyping words and gross generalities — and thus demeaned them, however unintentionally. For instance, consider these observations published in four otherwise respectable national magazines:

- "Cajuns are nothing if not jolly." *(Esquire)*

• "What lives in the swamps, plays an accordion, eats crawfish, speaks French and rocks your socks off?" *(American Way)*

• "Boudin is a hot Cajun sausage that has become the emblem of Cajun identity." *(Gentleman's Quarterly)*

• "The Cajuns who inhabit French-accented southwest Louisiana feast on crayfish and gumbo, hunt for alligators, dance exuberantly and revel in Mardi Gras." *(Town & Country)*

The false impressions conveyed by some media to the American public are an annoyance and embarrassment to the Cajun people. They also tend to hurt south Louisiana's prospects for industrial expansion and job creation, which are sorely needed here since the depression in the oil industry began in the early 1980s. Many of the stories depict the people of this area as much more interested in playing than working. Some out-of-state companies that might otherwise consider locating businesses here don't even consider this part of the country because they have been given the impression that the local people can't possibly be top-notch, productive workers. After all, how can someone who's been up partying and drinking half the night be bright-eyed and enthusiastic about his job the next morning?

The simple truth is that Cajuns in general are good workers They are a people with a heritage of tenacity and self-sufficiency. They own a tradition of excellence in boat-building, in agricultural endeavors and in the culinary arts, among other things.

Two books with the wrong titles

The inaccuracies and distortions that have created an image problem for the Cajuns are found not only in magazines and newspapers, but also in books and movies, and sometimes TV news features and documentary films. The most common problem with these works is their over-emphasis upon the quaint, the off-beat, the out-moded — without putting these things into their proper perspective.

One such case is a book of pictures mis-named "Today's Cajuns," published in 1980. It was photographed and edited by a photographer named Philip Gould, a Californian who moved to Louisiana and spent a considerable amount of time taking the pictures and interviewing his subjects.

The photographs in the book are pretty good as individual pictures go. But collectively the group of pictures he uses is as misleading as anything ever published on the Cajuns — given the title of the book, "Today's Cajuns." This group of pictures makes south Louisiana look like a Third World country. To look at some of them, you'd swear that the Cajuns never made it out of the 18th century! The book shows south Louisianians engaged in some unique, old-fashioned customs and traditional activities, and it tries to pass these people off as being representative of "Today's Cajuns."

The problem is, the title of the book is misleading. It's a half-truth at best but more like a one-tenth-truth! Had it been titled something like "Some of Today's Cajuns" or "Some Unique Aspects of Life in Cajun Country," then it would have been accurate — and would not have done a disservice to the Cajun people.

For the title to have held up as being accurate, the book would have had to also show bankers and business people in suits, inventors and entrepreneurs and financial experts, the body-builders from this area who have won the Mr. Universe title, the outstanding professional athletes like Bobby Hebert of the New Orleans Saints and Ron Guidry of the New York Yankees, some of the many children who attend the schools for the gifted and talented, the magnificent orators who speak from the stump and the pulpit, the painters and artists of international renown, the outstanding Cajun cooks and chefs, the women of timeless and classic beauty who have won in national and international beauty competition, and the everyday people who make up the bulk of the Cajun population, who put their pants on one leg at a time and who eat at McDonald's twice a month and go to school or to work daily like the rest of the people in America. These are today's Cajuns.

The people shown in Gould's book are also some of the Cajuns of today. And they are good people. They are people at work and at play and at prayer.

The book of about 140 pages emphasizes the kind of work and other activities that Cajuns have been involved in for a century or more: fishing, shrimping, crawfishing, trapping, farming. But it fails to include occupations like teaching and preaching, selling and counseling, computer programming and financial planning. Today's Cajuns work in the latter fields much more than in the former.

Two of the most brutal and disturbing images in the book involve activities practiced by only a small percentage of Cajun people. One is of a trapper with heavy stick in hand looming over a nutria with its foot caught in a steel trap, with the cracking of the skull about to take place. Another is of a pig looking obliviously down the barrel of a rifle the instant before the man pulls the trigger, then the pig being rendered and all the gory details that that involves.

Gould's book is heavy with images of people dancing, drinking and playing music. It carries several pictures dealing with horse racing at a bush track near the little town of Carencro. It has 11 pictures of the *Courir du Mardi Gras*, a rural version of Mardi Gras in which half-crocked men dressed in ghoulish masks chase down chickens to be used in a community gumbo later that day.

These things are not as vital to the lives of today's Cajuns as they apparently are of interest to the photographer, who prominently presents these images page after page after page.

The significance of these social activities in the overall scheme of things in south Louisiana is debatable. If the truth be known, Cajuns are more interested in rearing their children right, performing well in their chosen field of work, maintaining a meaningful relationship with their Creator and pursuing a healthy physical state, than they are interested in going to Cajun dance halls, drinking lots of beer, betting on the horses or watching drunk men chase chickens.

So, the book is flawed with the same malaise as some of the television features and "documentaries" that have tended to play up those parts of this culture that make "good footage" — the off-beat, the dramatic, the visually sensational — rather than take the time to create a real masterpiece of a story about a warm, unique group of Americans who have managed to preserve some of their customs a little better than many other ethnic groups who make up this nation.

Another book of pictures that dwells totally on the quaint and the rustic is titled "Louisiana Cajuns," photographed by Turner Browne and published in 1977.

Browne makes it clear in his preface that the book is made up of pictures that reflect "many of the old ways (that are) dying out." But, how many people read prefaces and introductions in pictorials compared with those who read only the title and the captions and look at the pictures? How many people read only the title, "Louisiana Cajuns," and looked at the pictures and concluded, understandably, that these must be pictures of the Cajuns of Louisiana as they are today?

The photographic content of this book is very much like that of the book discussed previously. It features some rather gruesome images of a decapitated hog being butchered, nutria and muskrats being skinned, and chickens being plucked for a gumbo. There is also the standard image of the masked men dancing with beer cans in their hands at the Mamou Mardi Gras. Cock-fighting and *pirogue*-racing are featured. There are also the pastoral scenes of a 93-year-old lady at her spinning wheel, and a girl putting on her shoes on the back porch of a little shack in Pierre Part, with underpants and brassiere drying on a clothesline that stretches across the porch.

There's no denying that these are scenes from Louisiana and that some of them still exist. But to say that these pictures are a fair representation of "Louisiana Cajuns" of today would be a mile away from what is true and accurate.

Movie-makers haven't done Cajuns any favors

The Cajun country of south Louisiana is a colorful place, no doubt. You just don't find people, culture and landscape quite like this anywhere else in the U.S.A. That's why some movie-makers have selected this area as the setting for their films.

The Atchafalaya Basin swamp, the nation's second largest swampland wilderness, has caught the fancy of a number of movie-makers. In fact, the swamp is so photogenic, so different-looking, that the maker of the movie, "Southern Comfort," used it as a setting from the beginning of his film until the end. He must have figured that strong, exotic scenery could carry a weak screenplay. Besides the preponderance of swamp scenery, the film's other distinguishing characteristics were non-stop violence and continuous vulgarity.

The story line is that a small group of Louisiana National Guardsmen are out on maneuvers in the swamp one weekend in 1973. They come upon a bayou they aren't expecting and can't cross without swimming, so they borrow some Cajuns' *pirogues* without asking. They're only a little ways from shore when the Cajuns show up. The Cajuns, who are considered the bad guys, are dressed up to look like something from the previous century. One of the guardsmen, the practical joker in the bunch, fires an automatic weapon — filled with blanks — at the Cajuns, and they dive for cover. The other guardsmen have the sense to know they're in trouble, and none of them are laughing now, especially the one who gets a bullet through the brain then and there. The weekend soldiers flip the *pirogues* over, make their way to the shore opposite the Cajuns and take cover with much haste.

Of course, they can't radio for help because the radio went down when the boats went over. The adventure in the treacherous swamp is heightened by the fact that the soldiers don't know which way to go, since the compass, too, is at the bottom of the bayou. Now the adventure really begins as the guardsmen are tracked and killed, one by one, as they try to find their way back to civilization. One of the men is stabbed to death by a fellow guardsman in a dispute over how to treat a Cajun "prisoner of war," another sinks into quicksand, one is snatched away in the night and hung, a few die of gunshot wounds. Two survive, by the barest.

Toward the end of the movie, the two survivors locate a road, spot an old truck and hitch a ride to a small Cajun village. As they approach, the air becomes filled with the unmistakable sounds of old-time Cajun music. Inside the bar there is a dance going on. The band is there, and the people are dancing about without a care in the world. Inside the beer is flowing, and outside the blood is flowing from a pig whose throat was cut after being shot between the eyes. A *boucherie* (hog butchering) has begun, to add to the festive air.

So, these are the Cajuns, as depicted in this movie — crude and hedonistic, barbaric and uncivilized, vengeful and murderous. But otherwise, a nice bunch of people.

On the lighter side, a movie that raised the eyebrows of more than one south Louisianian was "The Big Easy," starring Dennis Quaid. The movie is set in New Orleans, which Quaid tells us is nicknamed "The Big Easy." Presumably, this is New Orleans' response to New York City calling itself "The Big Apple."

Incidentally, New Orleans, which is a city in a class by itself and sometimes in a world all its own, is not part of the Cajun country. The city was, however, the port of entry into Louisiana for hundreds of Acadians who were exiled from Nova Scotia in the 1700s.

"The Big Easy" isn't what you'd call a real affront to the Cajuns, but it does contain lines that support some of the stereotypes about which Cajuns complain, such as the food being spicy and the people being party animals.

Mostly, it is amusing to hear Quaid and some of the actresses trying to talk in a Cajun accent. Quaid does a good job of acting otherwise, but, poor thing, he slaughters the accent. For one thing, he kept missing the Cajun word, *chère*, an affectionate term meaning dear, when he was addressing the woman he was courting. In Cajun French, it's pronounced "shaa," like the first syllable of Shasta Cola. But he kept pronouncing it "share," which would have been altogether correct if he had been addressing Cher Bono, the singer and actress.

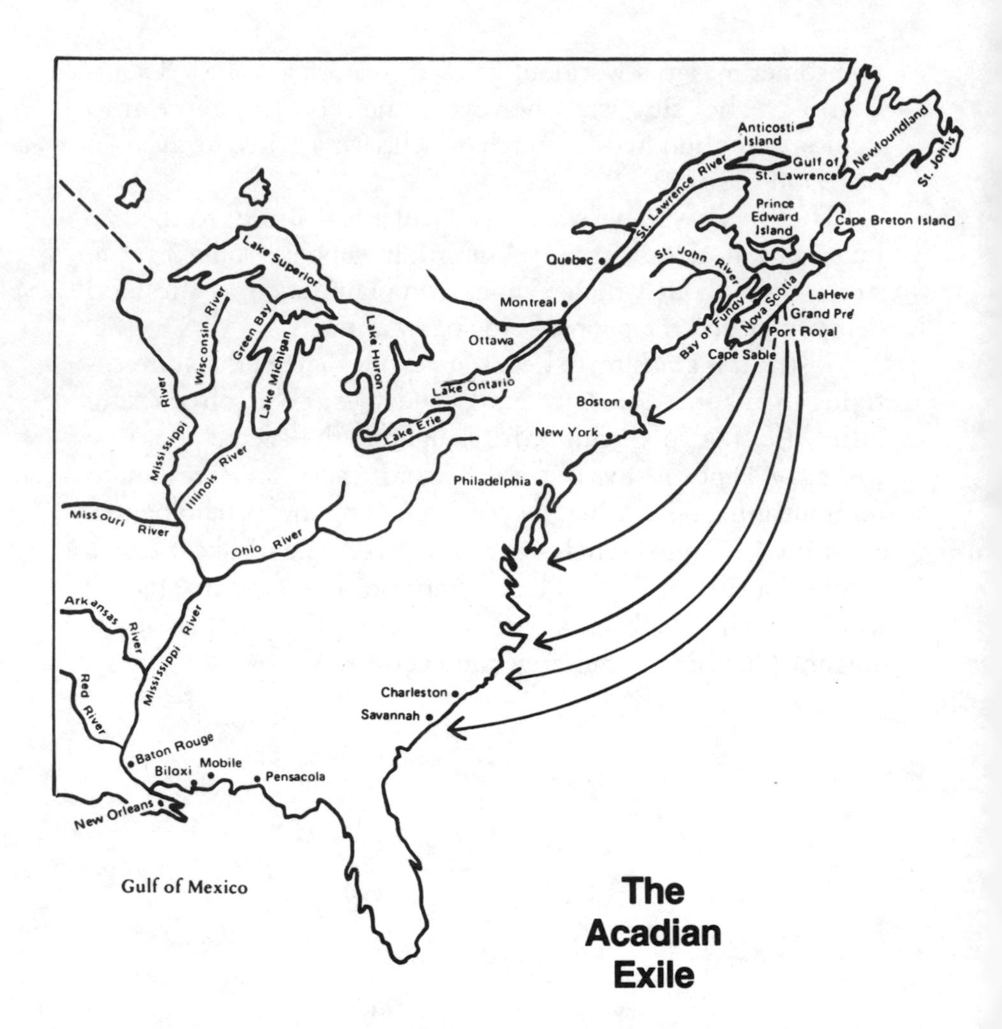

The French-Acadian people, whose descendants were to become known as "Cajuns" many years later, were exiled from Nova Scotia for political reasons, starting in 1755. They were rounded up at gunpoint, loaded onto ships like cattle and scattered all along the Eastern Seaboard. When they arrived, they were treated in an unfriendly and often hostile manner by the British colonists. Subsequently, thousands of Acadians headed to Louisiana and settled the area west of New Orleans known today as Acadiana, or Cajun Country. *(See other maps, pages 56 and 58.)*

Chapter Two

Who Are The Cajuns, Anyway, And What Are They Doing In South Louisiana?

LIKE VIRTUALLY EVERY other group of people who make up the population of Louisiana, the Cajuns, or Acadians, are immigrants from another land. They are from Nova Scotia, which is a part of the area once known as Acadia, or *L'Acadie* in French. In the seventeenth and eighteenth centuries, the land of Acadia included Nova Scotia, New Brunswick, Prince Edward Island and part of what is now the state of Maine. Most of the original Acadians immigrated from France, particularly those who settled in Nova Scotia.

The word "Cajun" is derived from Acadian. It came into being gradually, as a result of Louisianians misprounouncing "Acadian." They would say what sounded like "Acajin," then the first "A" was dropped to shorten it even further. Thus was born "Cajin" or "Cajun."

When the word Cajun first came into being it was a neutral term, neither complimentary nor demeaning. Later, however, it evolved into a word whose connotation was anything but flattering. Roughly from 1870 to 1970, when a person was referred to as a Cajun, it meant he was an uneducated, crude, somewhat uncivilized swamp-dwelling type. Happily, that has changed now, at least in most quarters, and the word Cajun is again a neutral term, just a shorter way of saying Acadian.

If the Cajuns of the nineteenth and twentieth centuries felt the sting of ethnic slurs at the hands of their fellow Louisianians, their ancestors suffered even crueler treatment at the hands of the British in the eighteenth century.

The Acadian Exile

The first Acadians were French Catholics who made a living fishing, farming and/or trapping. They began to settle the Acadian Peninsula (Nova Scotia) in 1605 — 15 years before the Pilgrims landed at Plymouth Rock, Mass. Except for a few scrapes and scrimmages with the British and some hostile groups of Native Americans, these French-Acadians lived in peace and relative comfort for several generations. They enjoyed good relations with the Micmac tribe, who sided with them in battles and taught them much about the land and how to live in harmony with it.

However, the French-Acadians' security was shaken to the

foundation in 1713, when Acadia was ceded to Great Britain by France in the Treaty of Utrecht, which ended Queen Anne's War. Predictably, the French-Acadians did not submit well to British rule. British authorities considered expelling them from Nova Scotia a few years after they acquired it, but held back because they needed the French to supply the British colonists there with the food necessary to sustain life. But as the area became more populated with their own people, the British became stronger, better established and generally more self-sufficient in all their needs, so they didn't need the Acadians anymore. During these years, the British were trying to impose their Protestant religion on the Catholic French-Acadians, and the latter were resisting. Most also resisted signing oaths of allegiance to the new rulers of their homeland. Their hearts belonged to France in the same manner as their religious loyalty was to the Catholic Church.

Though the treaty of 1713 allowed the Acadians the freedom to leave Nova Scotia if they so wished, they were customarily denied permission to go. The religious and political oppression proved too much for many Acadians, so approximately 6,000 left Nova Scotia secretly between 1713 and 1755. They headed west, into French territory, or north, to Prince Edward Island and Cape Breton Island.

The notoriously cruel Charles Lawrence took over as governor of the area in 1753 and immediately began making plans to expel the French-Acadians. He didn't want to allow them to go to Canada because they would increase the number of French people already there, thus posing an increased military threat to the British in Acadia. So he decided to round them up at gunpoint, put them on ships and scatter them along the Eastern Seaboard.

Governor Lawrence secretly arranged for the necessary ships. He sent troops to wait near the main communities. Then he issued an order for all French-Acadians to assemble at the fort nearest them to hear an official announcement. It was August 1, 1755. The announcement was that they were all under arrest, that they would be deported, and that their land, homes and livestock were to be considered confiscated, effective immediately. They were allowed to take a few belongings with them, but no more than they could carry.

Some of the Acadians were not in the groups who gathered in the forts, so the soldiers went to round them up. Many were tracked down and captured, but others escaped, hid in the woods and fled to Canada. Hundreds made it, but hundreds of others — without weapons, food or proper clothing — died en route.

What happened to the Acadians who were captured and deported was, in many cases, a worse fate. Men were herded onto the ships first as their wives and children looked on in horror. Some historians maintain that the British purposely split up the families to break their spirits and thus subdue the Acadians even further. After all, a man concerned with finding his lost wife and children would be too busy to take up arms against the British.

In all, some 10,000 Acadians were arrested, imprisoned and deported over an eight-year period, starting in August of 1755.

Some of the ships were not seaworthy, and they sank in the Atlantic with hundreds of innocent Acadians aboard. By and large, the food and water on board were inadequate, with the water sometimes being contaminated. The Acadians were crammed onto the overcrowded boats like cattle. Smallpox broke out on some of the ships, and hundreds died as a result.

Some Acadians were dropped off in Boston, others in New York, Pennsylvania, the Carolinas and Georgia. The local officials in the port cities of all these colonies were not happy to see the Acadians; they had not been informed that they were coming, so they were not prepared to receive them nor to accommodate them. Some Acadians were made into indentured servants and put to work as farm workers, maids and the like. In some cases, the children were taken away from their mothers to be brought up as Protestants in the homes of British families.

Authorities in Virginia refused to let the Acadians land at all, so they were re-routed to England and treated as prisoners of war.

In virtually all the colonies, the British authorities and townspeople were inhospitable if not hostile to the French-Acadians. Understandably, the Acadians got out of this environment as soon as they could. Most headed for Louisiana, which was populated largely by the French and friendly Spanish people. Others returned to that part of Canada which was predominantly French. Some went to Martinique and Guadeloupe, in the French West Indies. And some went to France.

Resettling in Louisiana

Of the Acadians going to Louisiana, some settled on the Mississippi River west of New Orleans near what was known as the German Coast (because of the many Germans who lived there). Others, hearing that many Acadian exiles had settled at Opelousas and *Poste des Attakapas* (now St. Martinville), went further west. They crossed the vast Atchafalaya swamp to settle in these communities, longing for the comfort of being with their own kind and hoping against hope that they might find some of their long lost loved ones. In some cases, members of families were reunited, but in most cases they weren't.

Fifteen years after the Acadian exile began, some 1,500 to 1,600 exiles had found their way to south Louisiana.

This group was to be joined 15 years later, in 1785, by the final substantial wave of Acadian exiles, a group of about 1,600, most of whom had sought refuge in France after being exiled to England. Their attempts to find a good home in their mother country had met with bitter disappointment, due in part to the lack of land to farm there. After long periods of exasperation and humiliation, the Acadians had been reduced to being wards of the state, to living on tiny government subsidies while the authorities continued trying to figure out what to do with them. Some of them appealed to the Spanish government to help them get to Louisiana, and the Spanish readily agreed to help. For one thing, Spain needed farmers who could produce food not only for themselves but for other colonists in Louisiana. For another, it needed more colonists for reasons of military security, since the British had taken over all land east of the Mississippi and north of Baton Rouge. The first of seven ships of Acadian exiles landed in New Orleans in July of 1785 — nearly 30 years after their plight had begun. Most of the 1,600 refugees settled at Baton Rouge, St. Martinville or in what is now Lafourche Parish.

The Acadians received land grants from the friendly Spanish government of the Louisiana colony. They raised cattle and grew cotton and other crops. They hunted and fished and trapped. They helped one another build houses and stores and small Catholic churches. They were surrounded by their own kind with names like Boudreaux, Broussard, Robichaux, Thibodeaux, LeBlanc, Arceneaux, Breaux and Dugas. They married one another, established community cemeteries, engaged in bartering goods for goods, loaned a helping hand to their neighbors and spoke the French that their parents and grandparents spoke. They celebrated Christmas and Easter the way they wanted to, and in peace. There were no British soldiers there to harass them, few outsiders there to water down their customs, for they were now independent and isolated from the world to the east by the vast and forbidding Atchafalaya swamp. This was home now. This was the beginning of the new Acadia.

For about 150 years, the Acadians lived here in peace and relative isolation, free from the influences of the outside world, free to practice their religion and customs, free to live their lives as they pleased. Many of the communities were on the banks of Bayou Teche or Bayou Lafourche, so naturally the people traveled a lot by boat. Generation after generation, they built their own boats, improving the design and durability all the while. This legacy has helped south Louisianians earn the well-deserved reputation for being some of the most highly skilled boat-builders in the world.

It was also during this period that Cajun cooking evolved into an art. Being settled in their own homes and having the time to spend to prepare truly delicious meals, and having easy access to an abundance of fish, wildlife, vegetables and fruits, the Cajun women of the day developed a kind of home cooking that is known and respected around the world today.

Cajuns enter the modern era

The long period of isolation began coming to an end as the 1920s and 1930s came around. Part of the reason was Governor Huey Long's road and bridge program, which brought much of rural Louisiana into the twentieth century and out of rural isolation. And the law of compulsory education, which went into effect in 1916, started taking hold all over Louisiana, including the heretofore isolated domain of the Cajuns. By this law, all children — even Acadian boys and girls — had to go to school.

There was bound to be conflict here, because the values, mores and customs of the Acadians were different from those of other Louisiana children. But perhaps even more of an obstacle to a smooth transition into the classroom was language: While some spoke French and English, a large percentage of Acadian children didn't speak a word of English. They spoke Cajun French, a language that had been passed from one generation to another by word of mouth. It may have been modern French when their forebears arrived in Nova Scotia about 300 years before, but the language had not evolved as it had in Europe and elsewhere. It was then, as it is today, an old version of a modern language. The changes in the evolving French language hadn't found their way into the everyday language used by the rural, isolated Acadians.

Thus burdened with a major communications problem, the children had a very difficult task ahead of them, though many did manage to complete their public school education. Their burden was made heavier by the ridicule and derision they faced from non-Acadian pupils who mocked their accents and in some cases their struggles to speak correct English. This situation was made even more unpleasant by the punishment they received from the teachers for speaking French in the classroom or on the school ground.

It wasn't only Anglo-American teachers who punished the children for speaking French, it was also teachers with Acadian surnames. They were taking orders from their superiors to educate these pupils in the English language, to help prepare them for life in the outside world.

Corporal punishment was the order of the day — kneeling on sand or corn kernels, having the knuckles rapped, the head slapped, or the rear end paddled.

Many was the day when an Acadian child returned home after school with tears in his eyes and welts on his backside to the sympathetic arms of his mother. Many was the time when an enraged father stormed back to the school to tell the teacher that if she laid a hand on his child again he'd kill her.

Tumultuous and often bitter times for the children, the parents and the teachers went on for years, and ultimately the effort in education did pay off. A new generation of Acadians emerged, far better educated than their parents, more articulate, with greater ability to help their own kind, with more real options on what to do with their lives.

This experience rekindled in the Acadians a renewed sense of identity, a new sense of who they were and who their ancestors were. It reminded them that they were different — and they began taking real pride in that difference. It brought to life a new sense of pride in their heritage:

We are Acadians, the same rugged people who settled the Acadian Peninsula, who withstood the severe winters that would have killed a less hearty breed, the same pioneers who cultivated the land and built the farm houses and carved civilization into an uncivilized land. We are Acadians, a people who were imprisoned and exiled from our own homeland because we were faithful to our French motherland and our Catholic faith — and we still are. And though many, many died, our spirits were not broken by the cruel hand of our oppressors. We have been re-united and have carved yet another homeland out of another wilderness. We have risen from the ashes. We are strong and resilient. We are Acadians. We are proud.

Proclamations such as this were made in the minds and hearts of many Acadians. Outward manifestations of this growing pride began to be heard in the homes as mothers and fathers had heart-to-heart talks with their children. Priests began expressing the same sentiments from the pulpits. School boys who had been silent before when ridiculed by fellow pupils began engaging them in battle during recess or after school. There was something happening here. It was the beginning of a revolution of sorts. The rallying theme was:

We are Acadians, we're proud of it, and we will not be ridiculed because we are different.

Politicians heard the rallying call and joined in, proclaiming the proud, noble heritage of the Acadians. State Senator Dudley J. LeBlanc of Abbeville, a full-blooded Cajun himself, began organizing bus trips of high school students to visit their ancestral homeland. They always stopped in Washington, D.C., and had their pictures taken in front of the Capitol, sometimes with the President. LeBlanc also wrote two books on the history of the Acadians, both of them glowing with pride in his Acadian heritage. The books sold well. One was titled "The True Story of The Acadians" and the other "The Acadian Miracle."

Picking up where LeBlanc left off was James Domengeaux of Lafayette. A wealthy attorney and former four-term Congressman, Domengeaux would not be content just making inspirational speeches on the French heritage, though he did make literally hundreds of them.

In 1968, Domengeaux founded an organization called CODOFIL — the Council for the Development of French in Louisiana. The creation of this organization marked the formal beginning of what the media popularly termed "the French Renaissance Movement in Louisiana."

Domengeaux used his considerable political clout to have the Louisiana Legislature make CODOFIL into an official State agency. CODOFIL's purpose: to preserve and promote Louisiana's French language, heritage and culture.

The focal point of the program was to have French taught in the schools — to re-do what the public school system had undone 50 years earlier.

For 20 years, until his death in 1988, Domengeaux put his heart and soul into the CODOFIL cause. Concerned that the Acadian culture was being diluted by influences of the Great American Melting Pot, Domengeaux often stated, "If you save the language, you'll save the culture; if you lose the language, you'll lose the culture."

This in part is what motivated him — a fear of the nearly total loss of the Acadian people's cultural identity, a type of loss that is not uncommon in the U.S. today. He felt it was a culture worth saving, and he believed that preservation of the language was the key.

He felt strongly that a grave injustice had been done, starting in the early 1900s, when the schools attempted to eradicate the Cajun-French language from the classrooms.

(Continued on page 49)

Some Acadians of Distinction

District Judge Allen Babineaux of Carencro is one of several dozen bilingual public officials in south Louisiana who are very proud of their Acadian heritage. Babineaux has the distinction of being the originator of the Louisiana Acadian flag, whose symbols reflect part of the history and culture of the Acadian people. The flag, designed by Thomas Arceneaux, was adopted by the State Legislature as the official flag of Acadiana. Babineaux was one of the original directors of the Council for the Development of French in Louisiana (CODOFIL) and is a past president of The International Relations Association of Acadiana.

Angela Bergeron, a student at Lafayette High School, is one of the hundreds of exceptionally bright young people who participate in Louisiana's gifted and talented program — which is recognized as one of the best in the nation. She works on her school's literary magazine and newspaper, is on the dance team and in the National Honor Society, participates in speech tournaments and maintains a 4.0 grade average. She's included in "Who's Who Among American High School Students" and "Outstanding High School Students of America."

—Photo by Robin May

Carl Brasseaux, an authority on the history and culture of the French-Acadian people, is assistant director of the Center for Louisiana Studies at the University of Southwestern Louisiana. He is also the Center's curator of colonial records. A widely published author, he has written 14 books on Louisiana history, Gulf Coast history, Acadian history, the French empire in North America and Cajun and Creole studies. More than 60 of his scholarly articles have appeared in professional journals in the U.S., Canada and France. He is also president of Louisiana's second largest historical society.

Roland Dugas is president and co-founder of Acadian Ambulance Service, which operates in 21 parishes (counties) in south Louisiana and is among the largest and most technologically advanced ambulance companies in America. While the level of success he has achieved is extraordinary, the same kind of entrepreneural spirit that drives him can be found in businesspeople from one side of Acadiana to the other.

—Illustration by Pat Soper

James Domengeaux was the founder and for 20 years the chairman of the Council for the Development of French in Louisiana (CODOFIL), a state agency dedicated to the preservation of Louisiana's French language, heritage and culture. One of the main goals of the program has been to teach French in the schools as a means of restoring bilingualism in the region; the program is succeeding, with an average of some 50,000 elementary students a year studying the language. Creation of CODOFIL marked the beginning of the "French Renaissance Movement" in Louisiana, which has helped restore and enhance the Cajun people's pride in their heritage and culture. Domengeaux died in 1988, but the program he founded is expected to continue for a long time to come.

Mary Alice Fontenot of Lafayette is an accomplished author of children's books and a prolific writer of newspaper and magazine feature articles. She is perhaps best known as the author of the "Clovis Crawfish" series of nine children's books. In a career that spans several decades, she has written hundreds of newspaper stories on Louisiana history, culture and characters, as well as co-authoring the book, "The Louisiana Experience: An Introduction to the Culture of the Bayou State." In addition to reading her books to children, she also lectures to teachers and others on children's literature, Louisiana culture and other subjects.

Ron Guidry of Carencro is one of dozens of outstanding professional athletes who were born and reared in the Cajun country. Guidry, a New York Yankees pitcher, won the Cy Young Award in 1978, which recognized him as the best pitcher in the American League, having won 25 games and lost only three.

Bobby Hebert, reared in the small community of Cut Off, quarterbacked the New Orleans Saints to their first winning season in two decades in 1987 and to their second in 1988. He played his college ball at Northwestern Louisiana University and began his pro career in the United States Football League, playing for the Michigan Panthers and Oakland Invaders. Hebert, dubbed the "Cajun Cannon" while in the USFL because of his ability to throw deep, says he feels a strong sense of unity with the Cajun people: "When I'm out there on the field, they feel like it's a part of them out there. It makes them really proud when something good happens. And when things don't work out, they hurt like I do. A lot of them do. I know that."

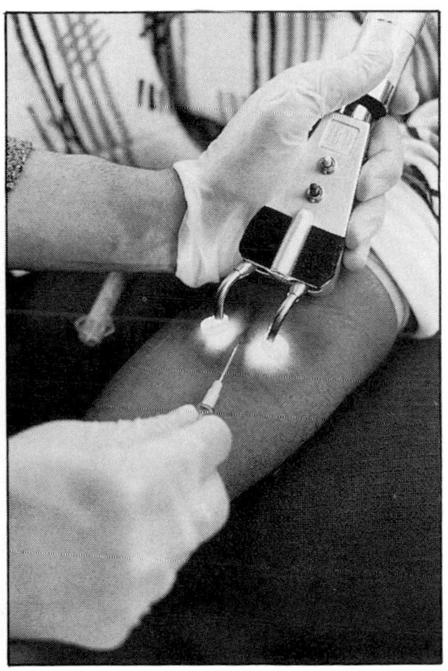

Dale (left) and Kim Landry are two of the hundreds of south Louisiana people who have patented inventions in medicine, agriculture, oil, fishing and other fields in recent years. The number of patents being granted to people in the Acadiana area is substantially higher than the national average. The Landry brothers, both registered nurses originally from Jeanerette, invented the Landry Vein Lite, which illuminates tissue beneath the patient's skin to make the veins show up "like roads on a map," so that intravenous needles can be successfully inserted in the vein on the first try. The device saves the patient the pain of repeated "sticks," lowers the risk of infection and reduces the hospital's expense of wasted needles. (The idea was brought to fruition with the help of the Louisiana Productivity Center, housed at the University of Southwestern Louisiana, which assists inventors with the patenting, development and marketing of their ideas.)

Dudley LeBlanc of Abbeville invented and promoted the vitamin supplement called HADACOL into the best-selling patent medicine in American history around 1950. As a state senator, he introduced and pushed through legislation that favored the poor and the aged, and in the process he became known as "The Father of the Old Age Pension in Louisiana." For many years LeBlanc had a weekly bilingual radio program in which he delivered the news in French and English and pounded home the message of the Cajun people's inherent worth. A folk hero and one of the most powerful forces in the annals of Louisiana political history, he challenged the formidable political machine of the famous Huey Long, but was nosed out in his race for governor. The late Senator LeBlanc was affectionately referred to as "Cousan Dud."

Benjamin Mouton of Lafayette is an up and coming movie actor who played major roles in two 1988 releases, "Sister, Sister" and a remake of the film, "And God Created Woman." A magna cum laude graduate of the University of Southwestern Louisiana, Mouton went on to graduate with honors from the American Academy of Dramatic Arts in New York City. He has several credits as a stage actor, including roles in "Look Homeward, Angel," "Julius Caesar" and "Romeo and Juliet."

—Photo by Denis Reggie

Dave Petitjean of Crowley, one of the top Cajun humorists in Louisiana, is a multi-talented entertainer whose credits include parts in about a dozen movies, as well as radio and TV commercials. He has had roles in "In The Heat of The Night," "No Mercy," "The Big Easy," "A Gathering of Old Men," "Belizaire, The Cajun" and "Houston Knights." He is also a member of the National Speakers Association.

Paul Prudhomme, who was born and reared in the Opelousas area, is without question the world's most famous Cajun chef. He's done more than anyone alive today to spread the word about the goodness of Cajun cooking — not only throughout the U.S. but to other parts of the world, as well. He is the owner of K-Paul's Louisiana Kitchen in New Orleans, one of the top-rated restaurants in the nation. He's been featured in every major food magazine in the country. He's been on the morning and evening news programs of ABC, CBS and NBC. He has some 10,000 newspaper and magazine clippings about him, his restaurant and Louisiana cooking. He has sold more than half a million copies of his cookbooks.

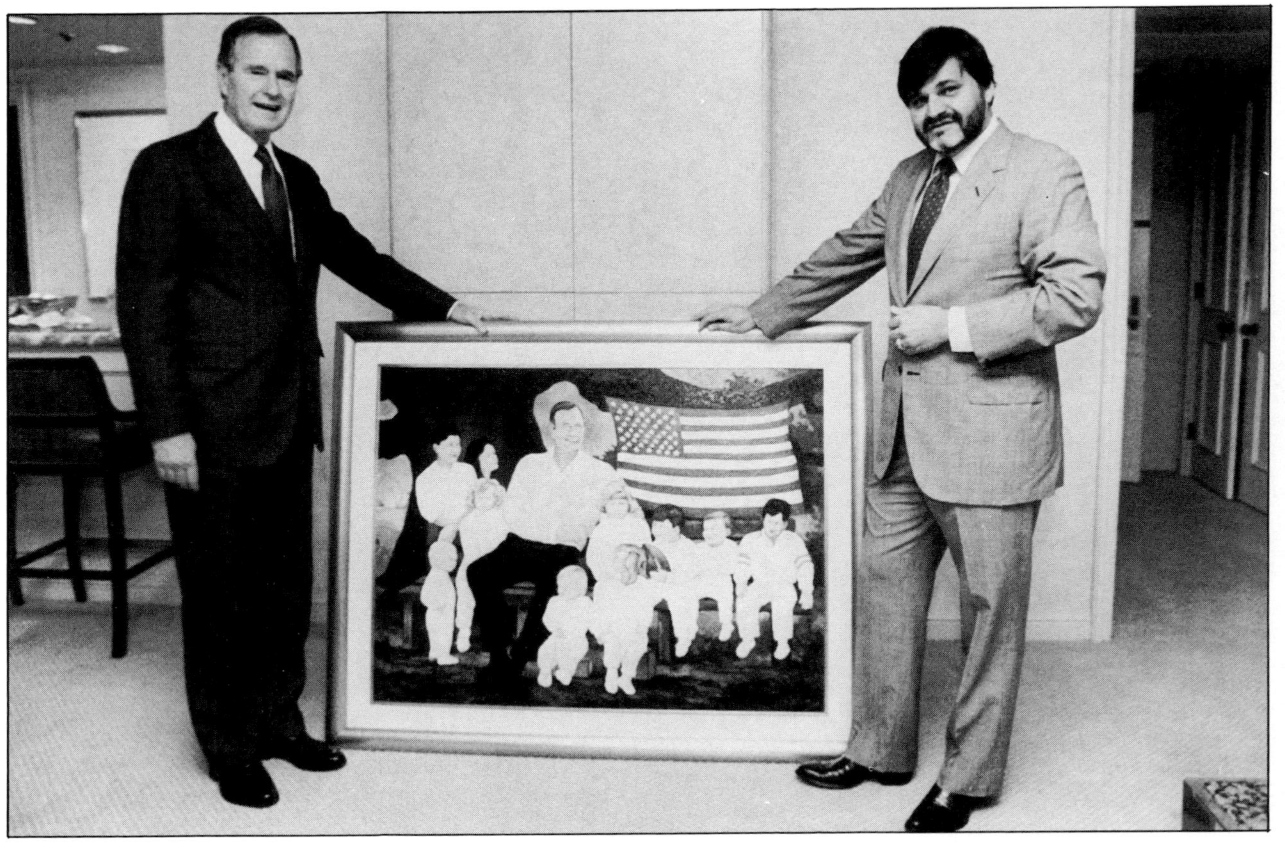

Lafayette artist George Rodrigue presents then-Vice-president George Bush with a painting of Bush and his 10 grandchildren. Bush said he was pleased with the portrait and reportedly agreed to Rodrigue's request to be the first to paint his portrait after becoming President. Rodrigue, who also did a painting of President Reagan on a white horse, is internationally known for his surrealistic paintings of the Cajun people.

Howard K. Smith, who co-anchored the ABC Evening News for seven years, has won every major award given for excellence in broadcasting. He began his career in journalism as a newspaperman, first with the New Orleans Item, *then with United Press and later with the* New York Times. *In 1941 he joined Columbia Broadcasting System as its wartime Berlin correspondent and remained with CBS for 20 years. He joined ABC in 1961 and reported there for 17 years. Down through the years he has authored three books and played in several movies. A native of Ferriday, La., Smith describes himself as "half Cajun," since he is of Acadian descent on his mother's side.*

Kathy Hebert Smith, a successful businesswoman and mother of three, was Miss Louisiana in 1968 and third runner-up in the Miss U. S. A. competition. The manager of an optical company in Baton Rouge, she is one of thousands of Acadian women who work both in and out of the home.

"The schools took French away from us, and we are largely responsible for this, because it was our own Acadian teachers who punished us for speaking French and refused to teach us about our language and culture — something that was within our right as free people living in a democratic society," Domengeaux wrote when he was first setting out on the CODOFIL crusade.

Domengeaux's motive in trying to return bilingualism to the schools was not one of revenge against the Anglo-American majority — though the more he thought about it, the more he seemed to be angered by the thought of what happened to him and other Acadian school children earlier this century. Rather, he was motivated by a love for his people, and by the realization of the value of bilingualism in this ever-shrinking world. He viewed bilingualism as a tool of incalculable value in international trade, understanding and goodwill. Trying to return bilingualism to the schools was his way of attempting to give a gift to the Cajun people and to other Louisianians.

While CODOFIL received some funding to implement its programs, the State of Louisiana didn't allocate anywhere near what it would take to go as far as Domengeaux wanted. So Domengeaux took it upon himself to find the money elsewhere. He had the nerve to ask foreign governments of French-speaking countries for assistance — and they agreed!

In 1969, Domengeaux met with French President Georges Pompidou, and Pompidou agreed to send French teachers to Louisiana to teach French, to help get the CODOFIL program off the ground. The French government agreed to pay for the teachers' transportation to and from the U.S. and for half of their salaries. Thirty teachers came for the first school year, 1970-71. Two years later, Quebec sent teachers, and two years after that Belgium followed suit.

In the 1974-75 school year there were about 230 foreign teachers teaching French in Louisiana's elementary schools. The number of foreign teachers was phased downward as more local teachers were certified to teach French, so that in the 1987-88 school year there were about 190 foreign teachers and 220 natives. Since the 1974-75 school year, an average of 40,000 to 50,000 elementary students have taken French lessons each year; the number for 1987-88 was 82,000.

Though Domengeaux is gone now, the program he founded is sufficiently well-accepted and well-entrenched in the educational system to assure its continuation for many years to come.

While south Louisiana is not a totally bilingual society now, the CODOFIL program has succeeded, as there are now tens of thousands of people in this area who can speak French. The French they were taught is the modern version, such as is spoken in Paris, rather than the old Cajun French.

There are also thousands of people in this area who still speak the old Cajun French, which was handed down to them from their parents and grandparents. Though this form is somewhat different than the modern version, those speaking the old French and those speaking the new are still able to communicate.

Some characteristics of the Cajun people

The subject of what characterizes the Cajuns of south Louisiana has been discussed for decades by historians, sociologists, genealogists, reporters, census-takers and others. Not surprisingly, they don't all agree.

They don't all agree on who the Cajuns are, much less what their characteristics are. Are the Cajuns people with Acadian ancestors on both sides of the family? One side? Or are they simply people of any nationality living in south Louisiana whose attitudes and customs are a product of the cultural blend of south Louisiana?

As used in this book, the Cajuns are simply people of French-Acadian descent; that is, people whose ancestors can be traced to the land of Acadia, particularly Nova Scotia, on one or both sides of the family.

However, the characteristics described in the following discussion apply to both the Cajuns themselves and to those who might be considered to be "cultural Cajuns," that is, people who are not Cajun by birth but who live in south Louisiana and whose attitudes and customs are a product of the cultural blend found in this region. (It should be noted, too, that while many Cajuns and "cultural Cajuns" share these same characteristics, it cannot be said that they all do.)

Strong ties with family and environment. Unlike the families of some other cultures in the United States, Cajun family members tend to remain in the same locale year after year and, in many cases, generation after generation. Because of this, they are able to draw on the strength of the family in dealing with the problems of everyday life.

"This is one of the things that really sets the Cajun apart from others in this country," says Carl Brasseaux, assistant director of the Center for Louisiana Studies at the University of Southwestern Louisiana. "We have that particular situation where the family is still here. We have a real sense of time and place — a real sense of belonging. Our roots go back at least 200 years. It's very unusual in this country."

Glenn Conrad, director of the Center for Louisiana Studies at USL, expresses a similar viewpoint:

"We in south Louisiana have an advantage that other Americans who have scattered do not have, and that is our families for generations have lived in the same historical, environmental context. So, it's a very easy thing to relate to one another, to relate to the environment and to relate to the historical background. Living in the same historical context is a binding agent. It ties; it binds."

Evidence of this binding — or bonding — is not hard to find.

"We hear repeatedly, even in these days of economic depression, young people saying, 'I don't want to leave New Iberia or Lafayette or Opelousas,' " Conrad points out. Even when the job dries up, the level of income drops drastically and the standard of living is lowered, many of them still will not leave their relatives and their homeland to seek employment elsewhere, he explains.

A spiritual outlook. People living in the Cajun culture seem to be less materialistic and more spiritual in their approach to life than the general population of the United States.

"They maintain a spiritual outlook. I don't know if I'd call it a deep religious trait," says Conrad. "But I think they still conceive of themselves as part of a metaphysical world... that there is more to life than just material things."

This spiritual trait is demonstrated, for example, on All Saints Day, when Catholics give special consideration to their deceased relatives, Brasseaux says. In a custom relatively unique to Louisiana, the tombs are cleaned, many of them are painted, and they are lit up with candles and adorned with flowers, he explains.

"I think you see less materialism here than in other parts of the country," Brasseaux observes. "That's not to say that people don't want their brick homes or their two-car garage and their boat. But I think you see a different value system here. You see people's ultimate goal in life is to be comfortable, not to accumulate tremendous sums of wealth. And you certainly didn't see the degree of conspicuous consumption here that you would have expected during the (oil) boom times. For example, out on the prairies, you see people who are reputedly millionaires and multi-millionaires driving 15-year-old pick-up trucks and wearing overalls."

Industrious and hard-working. The Cajuns have a long history of being industrious, hard-working people, dating back not only to their ancestors' days as farmers, trappers and fishermen in Nova Scotia, but to their ancestors' ancestors days as members of the working class of France. Today's Cajuns are engaged in a wide variety of occupations, and that same work ethic is still alive and evident.

Attitudes toward outsiders. The Cajuns' attitude toward outsiders varies from seemingly unconditional acceptance and friendliness on the one hand to extreme suspicion and outright rejection on the other — depending on what part of the region is involved.

Cajuns living in urban areas and having frequent contact with outsiders tend to be more accepting of outsiders, while those having less frequent contact tend to react in the opposite manner, according to Edward Joubert, associate professor of sociology at USL.

"There are very marked cultural variations between communities in this regard," he points out.

Joubert is one who sees "a definite skeptical quality about Cajuns." If you're an outsider, "you have to prove yourself" to be accepted into a small Acadian community, he says.

"Like any other ethnic group, Cajuns will not let themselves be taken over by outsiders," Joubert submits.

Louisiana genealogist Winston DeVille tends to agree:

"The Acadian has often been characterized as 'superstitious.' While that may be true, I believe that the word 'suspicious' is more to the point — intolerant of things that are foreign to his universe."

***Joie de vivre* (Joy of life).** This is perhaps the most misunderstood characteristic attributed to the Cajun people. It is an extremely subjective trait. *Joie de vivre* is possessed by many of the people living in this region to one degree or another, and not at all by others.

It is a very common misconception to think of *joie de vivre* simply as having a good time at a party. *Joie de vivre* is a disposition, a way of looking at things. It is not a state of euphoria that can be induced by the consumption of alcohol, as some have mistakenly surmised.

Joie de vivre is an attitude, a happy attitude. It is the ability to enjoy life, to really relish the good things that life has to offer. It is the capacity to interpret things in a positive manner, to find the good in things. It is the ability to feel real joy over the birth of a new baby, or the harvesting of a good crop, or the completion of a job well done, no matter what the job. It is a gift from God.

A person who has *joie de vivre* does more than just exist, but rejoices over his lot in life, no matter how modest. *Joie de vivre* is a subtle thing. It is a condition of the mind and of the heart. It is not always easily perceived in a person, but it is there as surely as the heartbeat.

Chapter Three

The Land Of The Cajuns

THE CAJUNS HAVE BEEN in south Louisiana now for more than two centuries. While they are not the only ethnic group dwelling here, their culture is one of the dominant cultural influences in the 22-parish (county) area known as Acadiana, or Cajun country.

In recognition of this fact, the State Legislature in 1970 approved an act officially designating the area as "Acadiana." This region, where the exiled Acadians first settled in the 1760s,

The Cajun country of south Louisiana, also known as Acadiana, is the land populated by the descendants of the French-Acadian, or Cajun, people. It is composed of the 22 parishes (counties) shown here.

forms a triangle, with its apex being Avoyelles Parish, its southwest corner being Cameron Parish and its southeast corner being Lafourche Parish.

The word Acadiana is forged from the words Acadian and Louisiana. Acadians and Acadianians are not necessarily the same. An Acadian is someone of Acadian descent, while an Acadianian is a person living in the Acadiana area, regardless of ethnic identification.

Of the 1.25 million people living in Acadiana, about 250,000 are of Acadian descent. Others include the English, French, blacks, Irish, Italians, Germans, Spaniards, Orientals and Native Americans. Many of these people have taken on all or some of the traits of the Cajuns, and the Cajuns have assimilated some of the traits of these other groups. The American Melting Pot phenomenon is at work in south Louisiana now to a much greater degree than it was 50 years ago — before the newcomers came with their new ways, before the interstate highways were constructed, the airports built, and the television sets installed.

The telephone books in most Acadiana towns and cities are testimony to the influence of the Cajun culture in this region. The books are filled with tens of thousands of French-Acadian listings such as Arceneaux, Boudreaux, Guidry, Hebert, LeBlanc, Martin, Prejean, Robichaux and Thibodeaux. The phone book in Lafayette, considered to be the unofficial capital of the Cajun country, has about 1,200 Broussards listed and 450 Boudreauxs, 800 Heberts, 450 Thibodeauxs, 500 Trahans, 300 Arceneauxs and 120 Babineauxs.

In the yellow pages of many of the phone books, Catholic church listings out-number the listings of any other single denomination, sometimes by as much as two to one or even more.

The predominance of the Catholic religion in this region doesn't fit at all with the pattern of Protestant domination in the Southern states. Neither does the heavy French-Acadian cultural influence fit with the pattern of Anglo-American cul-

Major Highways of Acadiana
X
XX
ALEXANDRIA
Marksville
Bunkie
Simmesport
Turkey Creek
Ville Platte
Washington
Mamou
New Roads
Krotz Springs
OPELOUSAS
Eunice
Kinder
BATON ROUGE
Port Allen
Grand Coteau
Henderson
Plaquemine
LAKE CHARLES
Carencro
Breaux Bridge
Jennings
Crowley
LAFAYETTE
Vinton
Lake Maurepas
Lake Pontchartrain
NEW ORLEANS
Atchafalaya River
Atchafalaya Basin
St. Martinville
NEW IBERIA
Gueydan
Kaplan
Abbeville
Donaldsonville
Mississippi River
Lake Salvador
Bayou Lafourche
Thibodaux
Lacassine Refuge
Grand Lake
Sabine Lake
Sabine Refuge
Calcasieu Lake
Bayou Vermilion
Bayou Teche
Holly Beach
Cameron
Creole
FRANKLIN
White Lake
Cypremort Point
Rockefeller Refuge
Rainey Refuge
Marsh Island Refuge
MORGAN CITY
HOUMA
Lockport
Galliano
Barataria Bay
Grand Isle
Gulf of Mexico
167
13
71
190
12
165
27
109
10
14
82
1
61
70
55
90

tural predominance. The existence of a thriving French-Catholic society in the midst of the Southern Bible Belt is a sociological rarity.

Since they first settled this land more than 200 years ago, the Cajuns, by and large, have stuck together, looking out for themselves and their own kind. As other American ethnic groups have done historically, the Cajuns have, almost instinctively, assisted and protected one another as a means of self-preservation.

It is in part because the Cajuns remained a cohesive and largely non-mobile group for so long, into the first half of the twentieth century, that their culture has remained relatively intact and identifiable. Had they scattered to the four winds, as, for instance, many Midwesterners did during the Great Depression of the 1930s, their culture and customs would have been boiled down in the Great Melting Pot of America — eroded and diluted to the point that they might not be recognizable at all today.

Ironically, it was the coming of the oil industry that enabled thousands of Cajun families to remain in south Louisiana. It was this industry that gave many Cajun people their first jobs away from the farms and the fishing boats — and their first big paychecks. Oil was first discovered in Louisiana in 1901 near the town of Jennings, and as the industry grew, so grew the influx of Texans, Oklahomans and others. Some observers feel that this influx of different people with different ways contributed to the dilution of the Cajun culture — or, put another way, to the Americanization of the Cajuns.

But, on the other hand, had it not been for the jobs provided by the oil industry, many fathers and husbands would have been forced to seek employment out of the state — away from the communities where their people lived, in some cases for six or eight generations or longer. The up-rooting and out-migration of thousands of Cajun families would have weakened the

Cajuns' influence in this land.

Acadiana towns and people a lot like the rest of U.S.

While the Cajuns have managed to retain their ethnic identity and customs more than many Americans, still they and the communities in which they live are very much like the people and the communities in the rest of the nation. The first-time visitor to the Cajun country should not expect to be astounded by some major differences he finds in the people and the cities of this region. The differences just are not that great, despite what he might have read in a tourism-promotion ad that proclaimed *Vive la différence!*

In fact, it would be difficult for a visitor to distinguish Cajun country from the rest of America were it not for a few radio stations playing Cajun tunes, some unusual-sounding menu items, an abundance of Acadian names on storefronts, and an occasional conversation being held in French on the street corner or in the coffee shop. True, in Lafayette, for example, you may see signs in front of businesses with names like Comeaux's Grocery, Carrol Guilbeau Tires and Prejean's Restaurant. And when you look at the menu you will find dishes like crawfish *etouffee*, crabmeat *au gratin* and redfish *sauce piquante*. And the waitress may have an accent that doesn't quite match up with anything you've ever heard.

But, besides that, south Louisiana is as typically American and middle-class as any other part of the country. Many of the same stores that line the streets of Atlanta or Dallas or Chicago can be found in Lafayette, Lake Charles and Houma: Sears, J.C. Penny, Mongomery Ward, True Value Hardware, McDonald's, Burger King, Baskin-Robbins and Dairy Queen, as well as large regional clothing stores, drug stores and movie houses — your basic American cityscape.

Some projects, people and programs of note

Contrary to the impression conveyed by some of the national news media, Cajun country is not a strange and exotic land made up mostly of swamps and marshes and little towns with docile, unambitious people who don't aspire to much except the next dance and the next can of beer. In fact, the people of this area, many of them of Acadian extraction, have completed or are involved in a number of on-going projects that can be accurately described only in superlatives.

Pelican Park, in Carencro, just north of Lafayette, is one of the finest, most modern softball facilities in the nation, attracting some 400,000 people a year to play or watch the games. Acadian Ambulance Service, with operations in 21 south Louisiana parishes, is perhaps the most professional, most proficient business of its kind in the U.S. The computer center at the University of Southwestern Louisiana is among the most sophisticated on the face of the earth; it attracts students from all over the world. The 12,000-capacity Cajundome in Lafayette is among the finest, most modern convention centers and sports arenas in the country in cities of similar size; it has featured not only a lot of big-name entertainers but also Mother Teresa herself. Red Lerille's Health & Racquet Club in Lafayette is one of the top 10 such facilities in the nation in terms of size and programs offered. South Louisiana is the number one producer of natural gas in the nation, and it is considered the "Workboat Capital of America" because of the quality and quantity of workboats, crewboats and the like which it turns out for service all over the world. Most of these accomplishments are due in no small measure to the intellect and ingenuity of the Cajun people.

There are some people in every ethnic group who distinguish themselves in their own fields of endeavor, and the Cajuns are

Family names of Acadian origin

Here are the most common Acadian family names found in Louisiana today.

Some of the names are also common among other French, but non-Acadian families, and even among the non-French. For example, Martin is typically Acadian, but it is also a French Huguenot surname, as well as English.

The names were selected from Bona Arsenault's *Histoire et Généalogie des Acadiens*.

Allain
Arceneaux
Aucoin
Babin
Babineau
Benoit
Bergeron
Bertrand
Blanchard
Boudreaux
Bourg/Bourque
Bourgeois
Boutin
Breaux
Brasseaux
Broussard
Champagne
Chiasson
Comeaux
Cormier
Daigle/Daigre
Doiron
Doucet
Dugas
Duhon
Dupuis
Gaudet
Gauthier
Gautreaux
Giroir
Granger
Guidry
Hachée
Hébert
Jeansonne/Johnson
Lambert
Landry
LeBlanc
Léger
Marchand
Martin
Melancon
Mouton
Naquin
Olivier
Pellerin
Pitre
Pontiffe
Préjean
Pujol
Richard
Robichaux
Rodrigue
Savoy
Sonnier
Thériot
Thibodeaux
Trahan
Vincent

no exception. For example, there are New Orleans Saints quarterback Bobby Hebert; New York Yankees pitcher Ron Guidry; Cajun humorist Dave Petitjean, one of the funniest men ever born in the South; Paul Prudhomme, the world's most famous Cajun chef, who has introduced Cajun cooking to millions. Additionally, there are countless other Cajun people who are masters of financial matters, inventors of oilfield equipment and machinery used the world over, and children of great intellect in the gifted and talented programs of Louisiana.

Following the difficult early years of compulsory education in Louisiana, the Acadians came to embrace education as the key to a better way of life for their children. Not only did they value and support the public school system, but they were among the leaders in building the private Catholic schools which are a major factor in the education of their children today.

Further evidence of the value placed upon education by Acadians and other Louisianians can be seen in the fact that there are four colleges in the Acadiana area: McNeese State University at Lake Charles, which has made major contributions to environmental science and to the development of agriculture; Louisiana State University at Eunice, a two-year community college for students primarily from a five-parish area; the University of Southwestern Louisiana at Lafayette, whose computer science program is among the best in the nation; and Nicholls State University at Thibodaux, a pioneer in the marine sciences.

Geography of the region

South Louisiana is in a semi-tropical zone, and it rains a lot here. As a result, it is one of the greenest areas in the country. Live oak trees, many of them draped with grey moss, are plentiful in south Louisiana, and in the spring the whole area is alive with the beauty of azaleas and dogwoods.

This part of the country is pretty well flat, but it has a number of uncommon geographical features. For one thing, it has one of the most extensive, most complex systems of waterways in the world; these bayous, rivers and canals are used for drainage, navigation, flood-control and recreation.

The largest of the much-publicized swamps of Louisiana is the great Atchafalaya River Basin swampland, which is about 17 miles wide on the average and about 100 miles long. It is teeming with fish and wildlife of many species. Some of the early Acadian settlers drew life from the basin, harvesting timber and moss, catching fish and crawfish, and hunting deer, ducks, rabbit and squirrel. Many hunters and hordes of fishermen enjoy the basin's bounties today. And, yes, there are alligators and snakes in the swamps.

Another interesting geographical feature of this region is the vast coastal marsh that separates the land from the sea. An incredible variety of wildlife lives here year-round, and their ranks are increased greatly each year as tens of thousands of ducks and geese arrive for the winter. Like the swamp, the marsh was a source of life for many Acadians of the eighteenth and nineteenth centuries, and it still is today, though for fewer Acadians.

Louisiana has been called "Sportman's Paradise" for some years now because of the great hunting and fishing that are the envy of the nation. The bass fishing in the Atchafalaya Basin is one good reason; another is the duck and goose hunting in the coastal marshes. Other reasons include dove and quail hunting in several places in this area, and the highly productive saltwater fishing around the offshore oil rigs. Also, horse racing is attended by many at Evangeline Downs near Lafayette and Delta Downs near Lake Charles and at various less formal "bush tracks" out in the country.

Louisiana is also officially called the "Bayou State," and for good reason. The presence of so many bayous in the Acadiana area is one of its distinguishing characteristics. There are bayous in the country, bayous running through farmland, bayous running through most of the main towns and cities. Many Acadian communities were built on the bayous' banks, since water transportation was the way to go in the old days. Bayou Teche and Bayou Vermilion snake their ways through the Cajun country, and dozens of towns can be found on their banks.

Perhaps the most interesting bayou of all is Bayou Lafourche, which dissects Lafourche Parish, in the southeast corner of the Acadiana region. Dubbed by local tourism promoters as "The Longest Main Street in the World," this waterway runs the entire length of the parish, some 90 miles, and spills into the Gulf of Mexico. More than a dozen Acadian communities were founded on the banks of this bayou, and the bayou was far and away the primary source of transportation in that era. It was, indeed, Main Street. Early Acadians traveled by *pirogue* or other boats up and down the bayou. Some lived in houseboats. Today, there are highways on both sides of Bayou Lafourche, running parallel to the bayou, and they are just a few yards from the edge of the water.

Bayou Lafourche has not been abandoned as an artery of transportation; on the contrary, it is heavily traveled by shrimp boats, oil-related workboats and recreational fishing boats. And traveling right alongside of the boats are the cars and trucks, usually making better time than the boats, but sometimes not. It's not hard to imagine how Acadian life must have been 150 or 200 years ago when you drive down the road alongside the moving boats and you realize that you're taking almost exactly the same route in your car as the Acadians did in their boats a long, long time ago.

The economic fabric

Another distinguishing characteristic of the Cajun country is the sprawling sugarcane fields that cover about a quarter of a million acres in the southeast and south-central parts of the region. The presence of the cane, sometimes 10 feet tall and taller, gives this area a bit of the flavor of the tropics, where cane was grown and harvested by hand for centuries. While the harvesting of cane in Acadiana has been highly mechanized for many years now, in some cases, such as when a hurricane has twisted the cane, there is no way to get it out of the fields except to send in people with cane knives to cut it by hand.

Slow-moving tractors hauling cane to the mill for grinding is a common sight here in the fall. And so are the fires in the cane fields at dusk as farmers burn off the excess leaves which are no longer of any use once the cane has been cut.

While sugarcane has been a major crop in Acadiana for well over a century, a crop that has surpassed it in terms of acreage planted and total cash value is soybeans. Farmers in the western reaches of the area specialize in rice, and the Port of Lake Charles is the nation's leading exporter of rice. Other crops grown in Acadiana include wheat, sorghum and corn and a variety of fruits and vegetables such as strawberries, tomatoes, cucumbers, eggplants and peppers.

Agriculture is a major part of the economic fabric of Acadiana. This fabric also includes the oil and gas industry, the petrochemical industry, boat-building, commercial fishing, food processing, shipping, retailing and a fledgling but growing aquacultural segment that raises various kinds of fish and crawfish in shallow ponds.

Tourism is also a very big business in the Cajun country. Next to the health care industry, it is the leading non-agricultural revenue-producer. The well-publicized Cajun restaurants are a top drawing card, but in addition to that there are some 400 other points of interest for the visitor to see in the 22-parish region.

These include countless Southern mansions and Civil War battle sites, picturesque beaches and fishermen's docks, tours of the swamps and marshes, beautiful old churches and an array of museums, numerous lakes and bayous and bird sanctuaries, quaint Acadian villages and rice and sugar mills.

Additionally, tourists are attracted by the hundreds of festivals and public celebrations that take place 12 months out of the year. There's always something going on. Incidentally, the tremendous number of festivals is one of the reasons the people of the Cajun country have the reputation of being a partying lot!

There are festivals to celebrate the harvests of sugarcane, rice, cotton, shrimp, crawfish, soybeans and much more — you name it. The blessing of the fleet or the crop is always part of the ceremonies, reflective of the region's religious heritage.

In addition to carnival rides, games, cake sales, live entertainment and the like, the festivals also offer a wide array of Louisiana cooking. Some offer boiled crawfish or shrimp, alligator *sauce piquante* and catfish courtbouillon; others may offer red beans and rice, jambalaya, crawfish pie and filé gumbo. Cajun bands and local people dancing the old-fashioned two-step always seem to find their way into the festival programs. Some of the festivals feature special events that are not found anywhere else in the country: crawfish races, *pirogue* races, alligator-cooking, muskrat-skinning and Cajun story-telling.

The many festivals serve as occasions for the people of this region to showcase some of the things that make Cajun country unique and interesting — the delicious food, the Cajun music and dancing, the often-present spirit of celebration.

Chapter Four

Cajun Cooking Ain't So Hot!

(But It Is Delicious)

CAJUN FOOD HAS THE WELL-deserved reputation for being one of the most delicious regional cuisines in the world. But, unfortunately, this reputation is being tarnished by some who have tried to glamorize it, commercialize it, and make it into something it is not.

One thing it is not is peppery. This is not one of the characteristics of good, traditional Cajun cooking. Another thing it is not is a quick-fix kind of food that can be whipped up in a flash or created by sprinkling on something from a shaker.

Cajun food is essentially good home cooking that is made with fresh ingredients, patience, knowledge and tender loving care (TLC). These are the real secrets of Cajun cooking.

It is true that some Cajun dishes may call for a bit more pepper than the average American is used to tasting.. But this is more the exception than the rule.

Who says the food is hot?

More than just a few food writers who work for newspapers and national magazines have slandered the good name of Cajun food by mistakenly equating it with hot, peppery food. To say that it is spicy would be closer to the truth, since spices are used liberally by some Cajun cooks — but even that wouldn't be altogether correct. But to refer to it as hot and peppery is just flat wrong.

This erroneous image of Cajun food has been spread also by some so-called Cajun restaurants in different parts of the country, as well as by some in south Louisiana whose owners should know better.

House & Garden magazine published an article in its August 1986 edition titled "Fire and Rice" and subtitled "Cajun cooking and the hot spice of history." Anyone living in south Louisiana and having grown up on Cajun cooking would know in an instant that there was something wrong with this story. And if the title didn't give away the fact that the writer was about to butcher the reputation of Cajun food, then the picture of two red peppers did.

The article, fathered by one Alexander Cockburn, is set in California and opens with the author and his friend talking about Louisiana cooking as they drive toward a restaurant that is said to serve Cajun food.

Once they are into the meal, Mr. Cockburn asks his fellow diners, "Why is it that these people would wish to eat either red beans and rice or dishes so hot that they can consume only a fifth of what's on their plate?"

Good question, but false premise. Fact is, most Cajuns don't eat food that's real peppery anymore than do most other Americans with good sense. Why obliterate the flavor of good food of any kind by peppering it up too much?

(And, for the record, red beans and rice is not a Cajun dish but a traditional New Orleans dish. Though Cajun cooking has had some influence on New Orleans cooking and vice versa, it is worth noting that there are three separate cooking traditions in Louisiana: that of New Orleans, that of south Louisiana's Cajun country, and that of north Louisiana. The three blend one into the other, to one degree or another.)

But back to the story and the restaurant in California. We rejoin the table after the meal and find the writer now pronouncing the inevitable, predictable, boring conclusion: "The food was good, but it was firey. The tears coursed. . . ."

Fewer tears and a little closer study of what Cajun food really is would have served the writer's best interest, as well as that of his friends, his magazine and his readers.

Another magazine that led its readers to the same false conclusion about Cajun food is *Gentleman's Quarterly*. In the February 1987 issue, the author stated flatly that Cajun food is hot stuff. The writer, Moira Hodgson, was reporting on the annual Mamou, La., Mardi Gras celebration, which involves men who ride around the countryside on horseback drinking beer all morning, starting at dawn.

Cajuns use "plenty of hot sauce" in their gumbo, she writes.

While it may be true that a lot of hot pepper sauce goes into the gumbo of these particular men, whose taste buds have been anesthetized by drinking beer half the day, it is not true that Cajuns in general do the same. Cajuns in general have more sense than that! They have more of an appreciation for good food than to ruin it by drowning the flavor in heavy doses of pepper sauce.

Have a Cajun Cola with your Cajun Pizza?

The issue of what Cajun food is has been confused by the sheer number of products called "Cajun" that have flooded the market in recent years.

Burger King had the Cajun Whaler (a spicy fish sandwich); Popeye's Fried Chicken has Cajun Rice (rice dressing with red pepper), the Cajun Catfish Platter and the Cajun Crab Claw Dinner; Pizza Hut came up with a Cajun Pizza, with "a special blend of Cajun spices." And, of course, half the companies in the country that make potato chips invented their own brand of "Cajun-style" potato chips. To provide the American public with something special to wash down the chips with, a Shreveport, La., firm concocted Cajun Cola.

With such a multitude of "Cajun" products being created, some people in the Louisiana food-processing industry feared that the name Cajun was being rendered meaningless from over-use. The State Legislature agreed and approved a bill enabling Louisiana food companies to stamp their products with a special logo identifying them as being made in the state. Not that that would necessarily mean they were Cajun in nature, but at least it would identify them as being made in the Cajuns' home state. Indeed, more than half of the 50 states were turning out some kind of "Cajun" food product when the legislation was passed in 1988.

Spice mixes and canned goods are two of the kinds of out-of-state products to which the legislature was referring.

For instance, consider Uncle Dutchie's Original Louisiana Style Cajun Spice Mix — with operations in Red Bank, New Jersey.

The company issued a news release of sorts in November of 1987 claiming that Uncle Dutchie's is "a great way to tart up an ordinary meal . . . if you're looking for real Cajun zing and zest." It went on the proclaim: "If you don't have the time and energy to prepare a full-course Cajun dinner, you can create an instant Cajun treat by sprinkling Uncle Dutchie's on just about anything you'd salt, pepper and spice up."

What's wrong with this message is that it implies Cajun food is a quick-fix kind of food, which is a false premise to start with. There's no such thing as an instant Cajun treat. Cajun food just isn't prepared that way. Good Cajun food takes time to make. It takes time for the ingredients to mesh one into the other. That's one of the secrets of Cajun cooking.

You see, Cajun cooking is home cooking that was developed by an agrarian people who had lots of time on their hands to cook — the way it was in the old days. They cooked with tender loving care, with pride in what they were to serve. They took the time to do it right, and to experiment, and as a direct result of this care and patience they gradually developed one of America's most delicious regional cuisines.

The notion that Cajun food is peppery is the other common misconception to which the promoters of Uncle Dutchie's have apparently fallen prey. The writer of the release proclaimed:

"(It) comes in two varieties: MILD, for those who like the nutty, peppery flavor of Cajun, but don't care for hot-hot; and HOT, for true Cajun lovers who want to burn up the bayous."

If the Uncle Dutchie's news release is not enough to raise a Cajun cook's eyebrows, a little recipe booklet that accompanies it just might be. It features a particularly startling revelation. In a short introductory message signed by Uncle Dutchie himself, the old guy points out that choosing which recipes to include wasn't easy.

"But I finally settled on the ones my family and friends voted as all-time favorites, (including) super-popular 'traditional' recipes like Blackened Redfish. . . ."

Hold on there, Uncle D! To call Blackened Redfish a traditional recipe raises serious questions about the qualifications of this panel of judges. Blackened Redfish didn't even exist until chef Paul Prudhomme created it in 1979.

Experts agree that the image of Cajun food has been tarnished

Two of the world's leading authorities on authentic Cajun food agree that the good name of Cajun food has taken a beating in many quarters in this country. They are internationally renowned chef Paul Prudhomme of New Orleans, who has done more than anyone alive today to bring recognition to Cajun food as one of the world's most delicious regional cuisines, and Marie Louise Comeaux Manuel, who was the director of the School of Home Economics at the University of Southwestern Louisiana in Lafayette for 32 years and whose life has been a veritable crusade to preserve the integrity of Cajun cooking, or "Acadian cuisine," as she prefers to call it.

Too often, Mrs. Manuel has given interviews to food writers and has been dismayed over the inaccuracies that showed up in their stories. So, she's reluctant to grant interviews anymore unless the reporter will visit with her in person and spend the time it takes to understand what she has to say. The writers just don't spend enough time in the area, or they don't know enough about cooking, or they just don't listen to her closely enough, she says.

In addition to the misconceptions caused by inaccuracies in the media, there is also the separate, ever-present misconceptions fostered by restaurants serving peppery food and calling it Cajun.

"When Cajun food was 'hot' (most popular), a lot of bad stuff was prepared and called Cajun," Prudhomme says, referring to the mid-1980s, when many restaurants were serving various peppery dishes and trying to pass them off as Cajun. Some still are.

The main reason why restaurants advertise themselves as having Cajun food is that they are under great financial pressure to bring in as many customers as possible. They need the customers to bring in the money to keep the doors open — like most businesses in this country. Unfortunately, some are much more concerned with the money than with the quality or authenticity of the food. They apparently feel they are running a business, not a cooking contest! It takes a lot less time and money to douse food with pepper than it does to allow the time for slow cooking, so that the ingredients can mesh one into the other in their own time.

Although he knows all about the financial pressures on restaurants, Paul Prudhomme's restaurant in New Orleans is not one of those whose owners hold profit in higher esteem than good quality food.

It was Paul Prudhomme who developed special techniques to make real Cajun cooking practical and feasible for restaurant use — an accomplishment of which he is understandably quite proud. Until the late 1970s or early 1980s, home-cooked Louisiana food was not commercially successful in finer restaurants, he says, pointing out that good Cajun food is essentially home cooking.

What held it back from being a commercial success was that many of the best dishes took too long to cook and consequently they didn't have the "presentation" that would be required in a classy restaurant, he explains.

"Long-term cooking is what gives Louisiana cooking that incredible taste," Prudhomme says, referring to the obstacle he had to overcome in order to serve the food in his restaurant.

So, through experimentation, he discovered that, for many dishes, that same home-cooked flavor could be created by cooking at high heat for a short period of time.

"This method gives presentation to the food that makes it

acceptable in restaurants," he concludes.

Another technique he uses to assure that his food tastes good all the time is that he uses only fresh ingredients, never frozen. He doesn't even have a freezer at his restaurant!

Recipes for real Cajun cooking

As Paul Prudhomme always says, good Louisiana food is essentially home cooking. Following are some examples of recipes for good home cooking. They were obtained from some of the best Cajun cooks in the world — the homemakers who run the kitchens in the homes of south Louisiana.

STUFFED BELLPEPPERS

—1 onion, chopped
—1 garlic clove, minced
—1 tablespoon of chopped celery
—2 tablespoons of bacon drippings
—2 eggplants (one if it is large), peeled and diced
—1 tomato, peeled and chopped (or one-half cup of canned tomatoes)
—½ pound of ground beef, browned
—½ cup of breadcrumbs or one cup of cooked rice
—4 large bellpeppers, halved and scooped out

1. Saute onion, garlic and celery in bacon drippings.
2. Add eggplant and tomato; cook until tender over medium heat, stirring frequently.
3. Add browned ground beef and breadcrumbs or rice; mix well.
4. Stuff peppers and sprinkle tops with additional breadcrumbs. Bake at 350 degrees until peppers are tender.

Note: Shrimp or crab meat may be substituted for the beef.

—Mrs. Ludovic T. Patin
New Roads (Pointe Coupee Parish)

CHICKEN & SAUSAGE GUMBO

—1 large hen, cut into 8 pieces
—1 pound of smoked sausage
—⅓ cup of cooking oil
—½ cup of flour
—2 medium-sized onions, chopped
—2 ribs of celery, chopped
—½ bellpepper, chopped
—1 clove of garlic, finely chopped
—3 quarts of water
—½ cup of chopped parsley
—½ cup of chopped onion tops

1. Season chicken with salt and pepper and bake for about one hour at 350.
2. Boil sausage for 20 or 30 minutes to get rid of excess oil; cool, then cut into half-inch slices.
3. Make a roux by heating the oil over medium heat then adding the flour and stirring constantly for about 10 minutes, until a peanut butter color is achieved.
4. Add chopped vegetables and saute slightly, about five minutes.
5. Add the chicken, sausage and water.
6. Bring to a boil; allow gumbo to boil two or three minutes, then lower heat and cook on low heat for about one hour.
7. Add parsley and onion tops, cook two or three minutes more, then turn off heat.
8. Serve with rice.
9. Add a few pinches of filé to each bowl of gumbo if desired.

CRAWFISH ETOUFFEE

—1 cup of chopped green onions
—1 cup of finely chopped celery
—¼ pound of oleo
—3 tablespoons of flour
—Crawfish "fat" (optional)
—1 can of chicken broth
—1 pound of crawfish tails, peeled
—Salt, black pepper and red pepper (Use sparingly)
—1 teaspoon of paprika
—Green onion tops, chopped
—Parsley, chopped

1. Saute onions and celery in oleo until wilted. Add flour and cook, but do not brown.
2. Add crawfish "fat" and chicken broth; simmer 20 minutes.
3. Add crawfish tails, salt, pepper and paprika; simmer 20 minutes more.
4. Before serving, add onion tops and parsley.

—Jeanette M. Guidry
Breaux Bridge (St. Martin Parish)

FRIED SHRIMP

—1 cup of flour
—Salt and pepper, to taste
—2 eggs
—⅛ cup of milk
—2 teaspoons of mustard, preferably with onion bits
—3 or 4 pounds of peeled shrimp
—Vegetable oil

1. Season the flour with salt and pepper.
2. Beat eggs and milk together; add mustard; season mixture with salt and pepper; add a little flour to thicken.

3. Dip shrimp in egg mixture then roll in flour.
4. Over medium heat in one-half inch of oil, fry shrimp for two or three minutes on each side until golden brown, being careful not to overcook.
5. Drain on paper towels or brown paper bag.

Serves six.

—Sidney Richard
Franklin (St. Mary Parish)

SHRIMP AND OKRA GUMBO

—1 quart of okra, cut up
—1 medium onion, chopped
—1 small bellpepper, chopped
—3 ripe tomatoes, peeled and chopped
—1 tablespoon of oil
—1 teaspoon of salt
—Pinch of black pepper
—1 cup of shrimp, peeled
—1 quart of water

1. Smother okra with onion, bellpepper, tomatoes and cooking oil.
2. Add salt, pepper, shrimp and water. Cook on low heat for 45 minutes.
3. Serve with rice.

Note: Don't use iron pot for cooking okra; it will cause okra to turn black.

—Mrs. Malcolm Guillot
Avoyelles Parish

Chapter Five

The New Age Of Cajun Humor or Justin Wilson, Go Home

WHEN I WAS A KID, I'D go hunting a lot with my cousin. One day we wanted to go hunting for dove. We were driving down the road around Lafayette and we passed a field. I looked across that field and I said:

"T-Boy, that looks pretty good to me."

Then I said, "I tell you what, man. You wait by the car. I'm going to go and get permission to hunt on this land."

So he stood right there, and I went up to the house and knocked on the door. An old man comes to the front door, a nice old man, and he says:

"Yeah?"

"Is it okay if me and my cousin hunt on your land?" I asked him.

"Oh, yeah, yeah, y'all can hunt all the property y'all want. I got doves everywhere," he says. "Do whatever you want to do."

Then he says, "But do me a favor. I'm old, I'm sick and I'm tired. I got an old cow on the side of the barn there. It's sick and it's old, it's served its time. Do me a favor. You got your gun with you? Please, shoot him and put him out of his misery."

"I'll be glad to do that, man," I said.

So, I'm walking back to the car and I decide I'm going to play a joke on my cousin.

I go up to my cousin and I say, "You know, that son-of-a-gun don't want to let us hunt on his land!"

"What?!" my cousin says.

"He's mad because we parked in his driveway. He don't even want us to take a picture of his property. Where's his cow?"

I cranked my rifle and — Boo-yow! *— I shot his cow.*

Then I heard, "Toom! Toom!"

I turned around, and my cousin said, "I got his horse and his mule, too!"

This little story by Ralph Begnaud of Lafayette is one of several he told to win the First Annual Cajun Joke Telling Contest, held in Opelousas, La., in March of 1988. The event was significant in that it was probably the single most rib-tickling event in the history of south Louisiana story-telling. And that's saying something, for a part of the country with more than its share of people who seem to delight in telling jokes and spinning tall tales.

Perhaps even more significant is the fact that the event was governed by the first ever formal declaration that certain kinds of Cajun humor were not considered funny, not considered amusing or acceptable to decent people, and would not be tolerated at this function.

While many, many south Louisianians have spoken up when angered or embarrassed by the performances of some Cajun humorists, never had there been any official statements issued by state or local governmental entities condemning the kind of humor that belittles the Cajun people.

But this night was different. This night someone finally got the message across loud and clear and at a public gathering. It was the Opelousas Tourism and Activities Committee, and they laid down the law in the rules and regulations they gave the contestants prior to the show:

"Tell only jokes that can be repeated in any crowd. Keep them clean, and make sure they are laughing with and not at any group or person."

The committee instructed the judges to judge the material based on these criteria:

"Was the material genuinely humorous? Was it in good taste? Would it appeal to people of various cultural, social and ethnic backgrounds? Did the stories typify the happy, open, good-hearted nature of the Cajun people?"

Not only did the judges seem to judge the material closely against these criteria, but so did the highly spirited audience, who packed the banquet hall to over-flowing. The audience laughed at the jokes that they deemed to be genuinely funny and humorous, and not at those that depended mostly upon an exaggerated Cajun accent, a silly-looking costume or a punch line that belittled the Cajun people.

By their response, the audience seemed to be making a statement: We are not amused with the efforts of anyone to put down or ridicule us or our neighbors.

The crowd's reaction to the entertainers is reflective of what seems to be something of a trend in south Louisiana: that the old-fashioned brand of Cajun humor — which relies on the exaggerated Cajun accents and broken English and which demeans the Cajun people — is growing increasingly unpopular with the Cajuns and with their neighbors and friends. It is becoming passé. While many south Louisianians may have felt compelled to laugh along with this type of humor no matter how offensive in days gone by, they seem to be feeling now that it's okay to not laugh, okay to register their disapproval and indignation.

The practitioners of the old brand of Cajun humor tell their jokes in broken English and contrived Cajun accents. In so doing, they spread the impression that Cajuns are simple-minded, unworldly, uneducated and lacking in their grasp of the English language. While their brand of humor hasn't done a thing to enhance the dignity of the Cajuns, it cannot be denied that there is some basis in historical fact for portraying Cajuns as unschooled and illiterate — because many of them fit this description a few generations ago. To a great degree, Cajun children didn't attend school until the State required them to in the early 1900s. The influences of compulsory education were slow to set in in rural south Louisiana in the first part of the 20th century. Of course, the same can be said of much of the South, the West and Midwest.

But even so, illiteracy is not a laughing matter. It's not funny in any language, in any age, anywhere, under any conditions.

Happily, times have changed, educational levels have improved with each succeeding generation, and today's Cajuns are every bit as educated as any group of Americans. So, the old jokes painting the Cajuns as illiterate are not only in bad taste, but also out of date and inaccurate — and should be consigned to the graveyard of useless material!

Justin Wilson doesn't represent the Cajuns

Justin Wilson is perhaps the best-known Cajun humorist in the country. He's been at it since the 1930s. When many Americans think of Cajun humor they automatically think of him. And they think about the strange way he talks when he performs. And many of them must think that Cajuns talk like he talks — in broken English, using improperly constructed sentences — and that perhaps he is a spokesman for the Cajun people. Well, nothing could be further from the truth. His contrived Cajun accent and the sometimes demeaning nature of his jokes have proven to be objectionable if not downright embarrassing to many in south Louisiana who take pride in their culture and their heritage. And they wish Mr. Wilson would just go home and raise a garden or something, maybe take up knitting or wood-carving.

For example, in one of his books, titled "Justin Wilson's Cajun Humor," published in 1974, he begins a joke:

"Dey got two fallow in Rayne in de Golden Peasant Cocktail Loonge. Dass on Highway 90, how-you-call, de Old Spaniel Trail. Well, dey got so dronk dey can't clam' down from dem stool, an' dass bad, you year?"

In other jokes, instead of saying "Come here," he'll say "Brought yousef here." Instead of saying "What is that?" he'll say "What that is?"

Get the drift?

"The mainest t'ing in life is to make peoples laugh," he is known to have told his audiences.

To make people laugh is a talent, and it is laudable; to make them laugh at the expense of the dignity of an ethic group is another matter.

This is not to say that he deliberately set out to harm or insult the dignity of the Cajun people. It is, however, to suggest that obviously he has been more sensitive to his desire to advance his career as an entertainer than he has been sensitive to the feelings of the people about whom he has been joking.

A new breed of Cajun humorist

A new breed of Cajun humorist is emerging, as evidenced by the jokes told at the Cajun Joke Telling Contest in Opelousas. These are humorists who are more apt to have their audiences laugh with Cajuns than at them. They are humorists whose magic will work based on whether the jokes are inherently funny, not on whether they themselves look or talk funny.

One such entertainer is A.J. Smith of Lake Charles. He had the audience in the palm of his hand throughout his presentation with jokes like these:

The Oilman's Bicycle: *Up in Basile, there is a fellow who manufactures bicycles. I went to see his place, and he's got beautiful bicycles — red, green, blue. I got to looking at those things, though, and I said to myself, "Something looks funny here."*

Not one of those bicycles had handlebars, and none of them had a seat, neither. So I asked the man why, and he told me:

"We manufacture bikes for them people in the oil industry who lost their behinds and don't know which way to turn!"

Super Chicken! *I was driving by Krotz Springs one day and I noticed this little fluff of feathers —* shoom! — *pass by my car. I looked down. I was doing 50 miles an hour.*

"What's this?!" I said. So, I speeded up. When I got to about 70 I noticed it was a chicken, just running on the side of the road.

Well, I decided to follow it, because I had to find out what was going on, you know?

The chicken makes a quick right, and I cut out after him. Then he turns into this driveway, and I follow him. I stop the car when I get to this house, I get out and I'm looking for him. A fellow comes out of the house.

"Hey! What you want?" the guy says.

"Man, this chicken just passed me on the highway. I was doing 50. Son-of-a-gun just ran right by me. I thought I'd come see what

was going on."

"Oh, that's those darned chickens. We're raising that for the fast food industry, you know. They've got three legs because more people like the drumsticks. So we bred them with three legs."

"That sounds good to me. How do they taste?" I asked him.

"I don't know. We can't catch 'em!"

Lester Gonsoulin of New Iberia, a man in his 70s, nearly killed the audience with his comical yarns, which flowed very easily, very naturally. He told the group that his "pilot light must have gone out" to think that he could go before an audience and tell jokes and expect people to laugh. But he kept them laughing all the while with jokes like these:

Accident Prone: *You know, when you dive in the water you go* bajoom! *So those little dives on the side of town where they sell beer and have a jukebox, we call 'em* bajooms.

Well, Pierre and Henri used to meet at the bajoom *every evening after work for a beer or three.*

Pierre comes in one day and both of his ears are burned. Henri says, "Pierre, what happened now?"

"Well, I'm sitting in the kitchen drinking a beer. Marie is pressing my shirt. The phone rings, I pick it up, but instead of picking up the phone, I pick that hot iron up."

"Well, what happened to the other ear?" Henri wants to know.

"That no-count called back!"

A few days later, Pierre comes to the bajoom *and both of his eyes are black.*

"Pierre, what happened now?" Henri wants to know.

"Well, you know Marie has been after me to go to church. That's a dangerous place, yeah. There was this big, fat lady sitting in front of me, and when she stood up, her dress was caught. So, I pulled it down for her, and she turned around and hit me in the eye — Pow!"

"So, how did you get the other black eye?"

"Well, I thought she didn't want it down, so I put it back."

Short of Memory, Hard of Hearing: *You know, when you get along in years, you forget things right away. You remember what happened 40 years ago, but you're not sure what you had for breakfast. But I'm not as bad off as that lady who went to the doctor and said, "Doctor, I got a terrible problem. I forget things right away."*

"How long has that been going on?" he asks.

"How long has what been going on?"

Pierre and Marie were celebrating their fiftieth wedding anniversary. Pierre says, "Marie, I'm really proud of you."

"Pierre, you know I don't have my earhorn on. Tell me again," Marie says.

"I'm proud of you!" Pierre shouts.

"I'm tired of you, too!" she says.

Another entertainer who elicited a warm response from the audience was Bob Hamm of Lafayette. At first he confessed to being "a red neck from north Louisiana" in his younger days, then he went on to make up for it with stories like this:

Heartly Sorry, or Hardly Sorry? *I've got to tell you the truth about Telespore. He's a good man; he'd give you the sac-au-lait out of his net. But he's been stealing lumber.*

For 12 or 14 years now, he's been stealing from Robichaux Lumber Co. That's the truth. He lives next door to the lumberyard, and every night he drinks himself a few beers, climbs that fence and gets him a 1 × 6 or a 2 × 4.

Well, he got to feeling bad about that. He decided to give back all that lumber and go to confession. He went and told the priest what he had been doing.

"You stole all that lumber?" the priest said.

"Mais, *yeah."*

"You ashamed of yourself?"

"Mais, *yeah. I'm ashamed of myself."*

"You ain't never going to do that again?"
"Mais, *no. Never going to do that again."*
"Well, Telespore, I think you gonna have to make a penance."
"Father, what you want me to do?"
"Well, could you make a Novena?"
"Father, if you got the plans, I got the lumber."

Two more funny guys

Two seasoned Cajun humorists who didn't participate in the joke-telling contest, but who are major figures in the ranks of the new Cajun humorists are Dave Petitjean of Crowley and Johnny Hoffmann of Thibodaux.

Petitjean started telling Cajun jokes to his fellow salesmen in 1958, and today he is among the top Cajun humorists in the country. Partly because of his mastery of the Cajun dialect and his experience as a performer, he's landed a number of parts in movies and radio and TV commercials.

Because of the pride he has in his Cajun heritage, Petitjean has modified his approach to Cajun humor over the past several years. He admits that in the past he and some other humorists depicted the Cajuns in an unfavorable, even demeaning, light. They were sometimes made out to seem like uneducated, dull-witted swamp-dwelling types. Now, he says he's making a conscious effort to portray the Cajun with more dignity, to show him as quick-witted and endowed with the strength of character and sense of humor to find humor in any situation he chooses — which is a mark of intelligence, not the lack of it.

Petitjean has tickled his audiences with jokes like these:

When Men Buy Corsets: My *friend Clebert went one day to buy some things for his wife. She needed one of them new corsets, you know, and he had never bought one. But he said, "I'll go try."*

So he went to one of those lingerie counters and said,
"Lady, I want a new corset for my wife."
"What color?"
"White."
"Short or long?"
"Long," he said.
"What bust?"
"Oh, it didn't bust, it just wore out."

Giving IRS Its Due: *I'm not going to tell you this fellow's name, but this guy wrote a letter to the IRS and he said:*
"Dear IRS: Enclosed is a thousand dollars. I cheated on my income tax last year, and I can't sleep.
"P.S. If I still can't sleep, I'm gonna send you the rest."

Mixed Blessing: *Onezime tries to help out everywhere he goes. He always wants to help out, and what happened, he had a friend that was real sick in the hospital.*
The man was laying in the bed with caskets on his arms and everything. He was in bad shape, and he didn't know if he was going to make it or not.
So, he said:
"Onezime, man, you have to help me out. I know I'm in bad shape, and I know I ain't been too good, but I have to know one thing. I want you to find out for me, if I don't make it, which way I'm going to go. Am I going to go up to Heaven, or am I going down?"
"I'm going to try to help you out. I'll check with everybody," Onezime said.
So, he came back the next day and reported:
"Oh, my friend, you are going to be so happy when I tell you this! Well, one part ain't too good, but the rest is going to blow your mind. I talked with the priest, the pastor and the rabbi. I talked with everybody, and definitely, if you die, you're going right to Heaven!"
"Well, Onezime, what could be bad news after that?" the sick man

asked.

"The doctor says you're leaving Thursday."

Johnny Hoffmann, a soft-spoken campus engineer at Nicholls State University in Thibodaux, has been entertaining audiences with Cajun humor for two decades. His routine centers on two fictitious characters, the always-unemployed "Uncle Noon" and his unattractive wife, "Aunt Mess."

Uncle Noon's attitude about work is summed up in this clever reflection: "Hard work never killed anybody. But, on the other hand, you've never heard of anybody resting to death either."

Hoffman has done numerous radio and TV commercials, and he continues to receive invitations to entertain all over the country because of jokes like these:

One Ugly Woman: *Uncle Noon's wife's name is Aunt Mess, and they don't call her that for nothing. She is the one they invented that old saying about: "Beauty is but skin deep, but ugly goes all the way to the bone."*

One day Uncle Noon took Aunt Mess to a plastic surgeon, and that doctor looked at Aunt Mess' face and said:

"Noon, I'll tell you what we're going to do. I think we'll start with her nose."

"What you gonna do with that? Straighten it out? Make it smaller?" Noon asked.

"No, I thought we would begin by putting it between her two eyes," the doctor said.

Aunt Mess Kidnapped: *Aunt Mess was down by the bayou washing clothes the other day, tending to her own business. A gang of fellows pulled up in a car, got out, picked her up and took her away. They kidnapped her, is what they did.*

Before the day was over Uncle Noon got a ransom note:

"Dear Uncle Noon: We have your wife, and if you don't give us $10,000 in small bills, placed in a shoe box under the bridge by six o'clock tonight, we will return your wife unharmed."

Drinking and Jiving: *The other day, someone at the bar asked Uncle Noon, "You ever drink enough to where your tongue burns?"*

"I don't know. I ain't never been drunk enough to try to light it," Noon responded.

Chapter Six

A Media Feeding Frenzy

SINCE THE BEGINNING of the 1980s, reporters have been coming out of the woodwork to write stories about the Cajuns of south Louisiana.

They've arrived by plane and bus, by car and by train from every corner of the globe, from every state in the Union. They have come with pad and pen and camera, all to get the scoop on one of the most highly publicized, most often distorted subjects in the media in America today.

Some of the feature articles produced in this frenzy of activity have been fair, well-balanced pieces that are a credit to the profession of journalism and a compliment to the Cajun people. But, unfortunately, a larger portion of the stories has been an embarrassment to professional journalism and an assault upon the dignity of the Cajun people.

Not all the blame rests with the reporters, however. Many of them are influenced greatly by what their editors direct them to include in their stories and by what state and local tourist commission personnel point to as being important. Moreover, they usually have only a few days to visit the area, and this shortage of time in itself can lead to superficial articles that tend to stereotype the Cajuns. Two or three days isn't enough time for in-depth interviews and ample research, especially when half the time is spent learning the lay of the land, driving to and fro, and sitting in restaurants or dance halls for long stretches of time.

For better or for worse, all the publicity has been good for the tourism business. Every tourist attraction imaginable has been written about again and again, from this angle and that. That's because a large percentage of these reporters are travel writers, whose stuff is published in national travel-related magazines or in the travel sections of metropolitan newspapers.

The number of tourists these articles have attracted to south Louisiana is incalculable. Authorities say millions and millions of additional tourist dollars have poured into the region as a result of this "free publicity."

But, along the way, there has been a casualty in this campaign to whip up excitement over south Louisiana's tourist attractions: The good name of the French-Acadian, or Cajun, people has been diminished. They have paid a heavy price for that part of the "free publicity" that tends to stereotype them as an unambitious, hedonistic, happy-go-lucky lot.

The simple truth is that the Cajun people have not been portrayed with the accuracy and the dignity to which they are entitled.

Too many articles tainted with stereotypes and inaccuracies

American Way, the magazine of American Airlines, ran an article in February of 1988 that was titled "The Time of the Cajun." It was a 10-page spread on Cajun and Zydeco music. The subtitle, dripping with stereotypes, asked and then answered the not-so-thought-provoking question:

"What lives in the swamps, plays an accordion, eats crawfish, speaks French and rocks your socks off? Aw, *cher*, you know."

Presumably, that would be a French-speaking Cajun musician.

But the problem with this line is that it tends to portray today's Cajuns as swamp-dwelling, French-speaking people who value music highly. The truth is that almost no Cajuns live in the swamps, that the majority of today's Cajuns do not speak French as their ancestors did, and that the vast majority of Cajuns just are not as excited about Cajun music as the author of the article seems to be.

In addition to running stories that stereotype the Cajuns, another common mistake made by some newspapers and magazines is that they run broad, generalized headlines that imply that what is to follow is a comprehensive article on the Cajuns and their land. For example, they run titles like "Cajun Country" or "The Cajuns of south Louisiana." As a reader, you'd think you were going to learn all about the Cajuns' history and heritage, their food and culture and their religious practices, as well as tourist attractions, geography, industrial fabric of the area and more. Instead, all too often, what follows is a story about touring a swamp or perhaps a long-winded dissertation on south Louisiana food or music.

So, the reader is left with the false impression that a large percentage of south Louisiana must be swampland and that food and music must be the pivot points of the lives of perhaps the majority of people down here. The net effect of all this is that the reader has been misled, and the publication has done a disservice to the reader and an injustice to the Cajun people.

A good example of this appeared in the travel section of the *San Antonio (Texas) Express-News* on April 10, 1988. The gigantic headline, stretching from one side of the page to the other, blares out, "Cajun Country," and the smaller subhead below it adds, "Swamp tour explores wild country of South." Two photos accompany the article, one of a tour boat in the Atchafalaya River swamp and another of people eating boiled crawfish.

On balance, the writer does a pretty decent story about the swamp and the people leading the tour, but the very beginning of the story is so close to fiction that you'd think it was written by Longfellow himself! It states:

"In one small pocket of America, a 200-year-old culture is tucked away in an age-old swamp. . . . The culture is that of the French-speaking Acadians. . . ."

This is patently false. The culture of the French-speaking Acadians, or Cajuns, is no more tucked away in the swamp than the culture of New Orleans is tucked away in a bar on Bourbon Street! The Cajun culture is spread out throughout the 22-parish area known as Acadiana, more so in some parishes than others; it has influenced the lifestyles of many in other parts of Louisiana, Texas and Mississippi, as well; and it has, to a degree, traveled along with the thousands of people who have moved from this area to other parts of the country.

Not to be outdone by the newspaper in San Antonio, the *Chicago Tribune's* May 18, 1988 edition ran a feature on the Cajun country and titled it simply, "Cajun spice." The subtitle: "In bayou country, down-home cooking and foot-stomping music preserve the Cajuns' grand tradition." Accompanying the article are pictures of three fiddlers and a stilted shot of Cajun food in a *pirogue*.

The writer makes the statement, "Acadiana is isolated, swampy territory two hours from New Orleans." What he must have meant to say is that in driving to Lafayette from New Orleans he passed by a swamp on the outskirts of New Orleans and later crossed over the Atchafalaya swamp, which is 17 miles wide. In fact, that drive on Interstate-10 between the two cities is near or through about one part swamp and five parts of other terrain, such as meadows, woods, farmland and urban and suburban areas.

A publication that makes more than one mistake in its presentation of Cajun country is *Houston City Magazine*, in an article by Ron Cuccia, in the June 1986 issue. It starts off with the generalized title, "Cajun Country" and the stereotyping subhead, "Touring the Land of Fiddles and Etouffee."

The article contains some excellent writing, such as his description of listening to the Dussenberry family singers near Houma:

"This, I promise, will be one of the most heart-filling experiences of your life. This is what it means to be human."

But, on the other hand, the story contains some writing that seems to be nothing more than a litany of stereotyping words sewn together in the form of sentences:

"Cajun country (is) the land of fiddles and etouffee, squeezeboxes and two-steps . . . where everybody's a cousin and everything's cooked in cayenne by a people whose religion is hospitality, whose devotion to passing a good time, *cher*, is one of this anxious world's purer states of grace . . . .

"Cajuns I think of as missionaries, come to this planet to teach us that fun is of the nature of ultimate substance itself, an ontological act of being. In other words, it goes with the turf. You exist, therefore you eat spicy food and drink saucy beverages. You live, therefore you sing, you dance, you laugh, you love."

Rarely in the annals of American magazine journalism has any writer come close to cramming all the stereotypes about Cajuns into one brief burst of verbiage. This is one of those instances.

An example of extreme absurdity can be found in the February 1987 issue of *Gentleman's Quarterly* in an article by Moira Hodgson, titled "Running Amok in Mamou." It deals mostly with the revelry associated with the primitive Mardi Gras celebration in the little town of Mamou, La. The story contains this stunning pronouncement by Ms. Hodgson:

"Boudin is a hot Cajun sausage that has become the emblem of Cajun identity."

Where she got this notion or who told her such a thing is not made clear in the article. But, for the record, boudin is not the emblem of the Cajun people. To imply that the lowly sausage is the emblem of the Cajuns is not only insensitive but also demeaning and degrading — especially considering the fact that, by comparison, the emblem of the people of the United States in general is the lofty, dignified eagle.

The Washington Post did a good job presenting a broad overview of south Louisiana's history, geography and tourist attractions in its June 8, 1986 edition. But the article, penned by staff writer James T. Yenckel, was tainted with two factual errors contained in a sentence that referred to "the spicy, pepper-hot Cajun food made famous by New Orleans chef Paul Prudhomme."

In the first place, good, traditional Cajun food is not heavily peppered, even though some commercial establishments choose to make their food hot and spicy and to label it Cajun. Just calling it Cajun doesn't make it so.

Secondly, while Paul Prudhomme has probably done more than any other individual to call attention to the goodness of Cajun cooking, it wasn't his efforts alone that made it famous. It had an international reputation for goodness dating back for decades before anyone in this country ever heard of Paul Prudhomme. Cajun food was made famous by the efforts of thousands of good cooks and chefs who prepared millions of delicious meals over a long period of time in south Louisiana.

One of the best examples of contemporary magazine journalism in this decade appeared in *Esquire* in May of 1987. It was done by Nancy Lemann, and it was titled "The Trials and Jubilations of Governor Edwin Edwards." The former governor of Louisiana was being tried on charges of fraud, racketeering and bribery, and, to make a long story short, he was acquitted.

Ms. Lemann's writing about the trial and the characters involved was generally brilliant, sensitive and very humorous. But, unhappily, some of her references to the Cajun people were insensitive and bordering on ethnic insult.

Her first questionable remark referred to "a rotund, jocose Cajun-like fellow of Greek extraction, Gus Mijalis (the jolly defendant)."

Now, the man may be stout and jolly and Greek. But "Cajun-like?" How is a person Cajun-like? Cajuns don't act the same way or talk the same way, nor do they share the same countenance or sense of humor. Cajuns are so diverse in their traits as to render the term "Cajun-like" meaningless.

Later in the story, in a section on the mannerisms of the governor's brother, the writer flatly stereotypes the Cajun people:

"Cajuns are nothing if not jolly."

What this comment serves to do is to reinforce in her readers' minds The Myth of The Jolly Cajun. This myth portrays the Cajuns as a happy-go-lucky bunch who, regardless of the difficulties that befall them, go skipping merrily through life without a care in the world.

It is true that many of the Cajuns of south Louisiana, living in the Southern United States as they do, tend to be hospitable — a trait often attributed to Southerners. It is also true that many Cajuns have enough of a sense of humor to enjoy a good joke, like most other people on the planet. But for Ms. Lemann to write without qualification, "Cajuns are nothing if not jolly," well, that's a gross over-simplification that weakens and taints an otherwise fine piece of literature.

Town & Country magazine article seriously flawed

One of the most sensational contrivances ever published dealing with the Cajuns is the opening page of a spread that appeared in the May 1988 issue of *Town & Country* magazine. It features a picture of seven chefs behind a gigantic alligator with a swamp in the background.

The trite picture is outdone in triteness by the headline, "Cajuns, Crocs and Crayfish," which, in turn, is outdone by the hackneyed and terribly trite subtitle:

"The Cajuns who inhabit French-accented southwest Louisiana feast on crayfish and gumbo, hunt for alligators, dance exuberantly and revel in Mardi Gras. But, there's another side to the rich heritage of Acadiana: homegrown oil barons, vast cattle ranches, grand plantations and a laid-back local aristocracy."

The one redeeming quality of the story's subtitle is that it makes an attempt at balancing or at least diversifying the image it projects by mentioning that some people in this part of the country are rich. Indeed, much of the article deals with the success stories and lifestyles of some of the area's wealthy.

Otherwise, what can one say about this opening page? How can one begin to address this frontal assault upon the dignity of the Cajun people?

For openers, to say that Cajuns hunt alligators is misleading, unless one explains that perhaps 800 out of 1,250,000 people who live in the Cajun country hunt alligators and that of this

800, perhaps half are actually Cajuns. From this it can be concluded that the vast, vast majority of Cajuns do not hunt alligators.

To say that Cajuns dance exuberantly is to imply, at the very least, that most Cajuns dance in this manner. In fact, while some do, many more do not — because of their age, their inexperience or various inhibitions. And many others don't dance at all. If the Great Cajun Dance Contest were held today and all Cajuns showed up for the event, there would probably be five percent dancing exuberantly, ten percent more imitating the exuberant, 30 percent dancing like grandmas and grandpas, that is, real conservatively, and the rest of the group sitting around talking about them.

To say that Cajuns revel in Mardi Gras is not altogether accurate either, inasmuch as many Cajuns, once they have passed the stage of adolescence, have no interest in Mardi Gras at all. Some don't feel safe in large crowds, especially where a lot of people are consuming alcohol and some are taking other drugs. Others don't participate because they want to avoid the post-Mardi Gras blues, that feeling of emptiness that comes after attending a big party where everyone seems to be so happy and when it's over the thrill is gone and the emptiness sets in. Others don't go because they are more concerned with the things of the spirit, and, with the solemn season of Lent starting the next day, their thoughts have already begun to turn more to prayer, sacrifice and self-denial.

When you stop to think of what the words in this subtitle are saying — that the Cajuns feast on crawfish and gumbo, dance with exuberance, revel in Mardi Gras and engage in the ugly business of tracking down and killing alligators — what image of the Cajuns could be conveyed to the readers of this magazine other than the image of a people who are hedonistic and brutal? The wording is misleading, the image inaccurate. These traits do not describe the essential character of the Cajuns, although many Cajuns do know how to enjoy life and, like their ancestors, have found it within themselves to be tough in their efforts to survive and to provide for their families.

Chapter Seven

Anatomy Of A False Impression

MANY AMERICANS HAVE false impressions of the Cajun people, the food they eat and the land in which they live. And little wonder. They get these ideas from all directions: from what they read in the newspapers and magazines, from what they see and hear on television and in the movies, from what they hear from friends who have been here.

There are several factors involved here, and all of them, to one degree or another, contribute to the creation of an image of the Cajuns that just isn't accurate. Some of the main factors are these:

1. Proliferation of distorted tourism articles on this area. In days gone by, relatively few stories on the Cajun country appeared each year in metropolitan newspapers and national magazines. But now dozens upon dozens of articles are making their way into print each year — and many of them are portraying the Cajuns and their land in stereotypical fashion. The reader who's never been to south Louisiana may have little or no reason to question the accuracy or completeness of these articles. Besides, how could that many stories be wrong? (Actually, they are not wrong, but they play up the food, music, partying and swamps so much that the other less unique, less sensational characteristics of the Cajun country are excluded — so a grossly distorted image emerges.)

The sheer number of stories, the continual bombardment of articles with the same common denominators leaves a lasting impression on the reading audience, as the inaccuracies in one article reinforce the distortions in the others.

2. Lack of balance and perspective in tourism articles. A large portion of the features on the Cajun country appearing in the media today is in the travel sections of magazines and newspapers and in publications devoted totally to traveling and sight-seeing. Far too many of these feature the same few attractions (food, music, dancing, drinking and swamps), to the exclusion of other attractions that some tourists would find just as interesting, if not more so. For instance, the shrimp boat docks in Morgan City and Delcambre, the gigantic offshore oil platforms (some as tall as 50-story buildings, and taller), the numerous Southern mansions reminiscent of another era, the site of the Miracle of Grand Coteau, the statue of Evangeline that commemorates the heroine of Longfellow's poem by the same name, the fine freshwater and saltwater fishing to be enjoyed in Louisiana waters.

There seems to be a widespread absence of effort by writers to put south Louisiana's tourist attractions into perspective. For instance, it would help to balance their stories if these writers would include a paragraph or two saying that the remnants of the old-time Cajun culture can be found alive and well and coexisting nicely with the things of modern-day Louisiana, such as contemporary multi-story glass-and-steel office buildings, interstate highways, regional and international airports. They could mention that Louisiana is the number one producer of natural gas in the U.S., the top producer of seafood, one of the leading producers of oil, that it has some of the most productive agricultural lands on earth. It could also be noted that south Louisiana is considered the "Workboat Capital of America."

The lack of counterbalancing information in these stories sometimes is due to the fact that the reporters didn't have time to dig for it, or they weren't interested enough to include it even if they had it in hand. Sometimes the information simply wasn't offered to them by the tourist agency representatives or others who guided them to the tourist attractions; or if it was offered it wasn't emphasized enough for the reporters to feel they should include it.

One problem of perspective that is easily avoidable is the misleading, over-generalizing headline. For example, it's misleading to run a headline that says only "The Cajuns," then a story describing only those Cajuns who go out dancing frequently or who are French-speaking. It's also misleading to run a headline that says, "Cajun Country," then write about only one segment of it, like the swamp, and imply that this is the Cajun country, period.

3. Tendency of reporters and editors to use stereotyping words and phrases. Some reporters use this kind of language because they've seen it used so often before, because they hear a tour guide use it, or because it seems to aptly describe what they're seeing. But so many reporters use the same trite, often erroneous wordage that one is led to believe they must be copying off of each other or perhaps interviewing exactly they same people.

For instance, they write that Louisiana is "swampy," while, in fact, swamps actually take up a relatively small percentage of the land in the state. They report that the food is "peppery hot" because maybe they've had some in a restaurant once, though this isn't an accurate description of authentic Cajun food. They refer to the "French-speaking Cajuns," when actually the majority of today's Cajuns do not speak French. They make historical references to "the rebellious Acadians," but the facts say otherwise.

More than one reporter has written that the philosophy of "the fun-loving Cajuns" can be summed up in the "often-heard" phrase, "*Laissez les bon temps rouler!*" (Let the good times roll). However, in the past decade this phrase has probably appeared more in out-of-state newspapers and magazines than it has been spoken by local people — even just before a dance was to begin. The phrase is more a product of journalese than Cajunese.

4. Insufficient time allowed for the reporter to be thorough. Unless the reporter has done a lot of homework on the Cajuns before arriving here, two or three days just isn't enough time to do a thorough, well-balanced article. Quick trips tend to produce shallow stories that tend to stereotype the Cajun people.

Unless he has done extensive research beforehand, no reporter can show up in a place, interview a handful of local people, check out the cuisine, take in the swamp tour, gather up a few brochures from the tourist commission or the chamber of commerce, then go home and do a fair, balanced article on the local people and their culture. And if he does write a story after a quick visit, the resulting story should be identified as such, either by an editor's note or by a carefully worded headline that says something like, "A few observations about the Cajun country" or "What I saw in south Louisiana last weekend." This way, the reader will see it as the casual piece that it is, rather than as the definitive piece that might be implied if it were run under a headline that simply said "Cajun Country."

5. Preconceived notions of editors. Like other people, some editors base their impressions of Cajun country on articles they've read, things they've heard, movies they've seen. So, when they're assigning reporters to do stories on the Cajuns and their land, their preconceived notions come into play. It's not hard to imagine an editor giving his reporter an assignment in words that sound something like this:

"Be sure to include something on the hot food we're always hearing about. . . and all the partying, drinking and dancing that go on down there. But don't get too tied up in it yourself. I need you back here in three days, with the story — and sober! And wasn't there something about the people speaking French instead of English? Look into that. Bring me some pictures of the swamp, of Cajun musicians and whatever else looks interesting."

With instructions like these, you can bet the editor's preconceived notions will show up in the reporter's story — thus reinforcing in the readers' minds that this is what Cajun country is all about.

6. Preconceived notions of reporters. Even without the aforementioned instructions from the editor, many reporters already have the same ideas about what the Cajun country is like — possibly from the same sources — so the probabilities are that these notions will be evident in the story.

Unfortunately, some reporters would feel comfortable including these elements without much examination of their validity — and without much effort to put them into a realistic perspective. After all, this is what the editor asked for, it's what the local tourist commission representatives said should be in the story, and, besides, these elements will make for a great article anyway because they're so different from anything the readers have seen in the pages of this publication in a long time.

7. Deficiencies in the photo selection process. Given the choice, a good magazine or newspaper photographer will tend to photograph subjects that make the best pictures — the scenic, the sensational or dramatic, the unusual, the off-beat. (This goes for cameramen who shoot for TV and those who shoot for print media.) They sometimes don't even take the pictures that are less interesting, less aesthetically pleasing, but possibly more important to a balanced presentation. This can be because the editor failed to be specific enough in his instructions. Or it can be because the photographer is so taken with what's pretty or unusual that he doesn't see what's important.

When the photographer excludes what might be important, or what might bring balance to the presentation, he narrows down the choices of what pictures the editor might run if he had them. In so doing, it is the photographer who has decided to a great degree what will be published.

Sometimes it happens that even when the photographer brings back the right mix of pictures, the editor opts to run only those that are the prettiest or most unusual. This may be because he doesn't have enough space to run more; or it may be because he is lacking in competence as an editor.

8. Narrowness in network news. Too often on network news programs the people of south Louisiana have been depicted as something less than bright, involved American citizens. The impression that can be made on the American viewing audience in five, ten or 30 seconds is powerful — and it can be lasting.

Louisiana genealogist Winston DeVille took strong exception to one network news show in August of 1988 in a column he wrote for the *Alexandria (La.) Daily Town Talk:*

"As this column is being written, the 'Sunday Morning' show (CBS) is on, featuring our state. One segment, inevitably, was on the so-called 'Cajuns' of south Louisiana. . . .

"As usual, national television chose to show primarily a simple-minded, child-like people who live primitively, and only for frolic. It's disgusting."

Earlier in 1988, when the presidential primaries were underway, NBC television was getting a feel for how people throughout the country viewed the candidates and the primaries. The reporter interviewed one of the participants in the Mamou, La., Mardi Gras celebration. The local man said essentially that he didn't know anything about it, and he implied that he cared even less. He came across like a child who just wanted to get back to the playground.

If the TV people had been sincere about wanting to know what south Louisianians thought, they could have asked a businesswoman in New Iberia, a sugarcane farmer in Houma, a stock broker in Lafayette or a school teacher in Lake Charles.

9. Movies that stereotype the Cajuns. Some of the movies set in south Louisiana in the 1980s have supported the stereotypes about the Cajuns and their land. Perhaps the worst offender was "Southern Comfort," which showed the Cajuns not only as ignorant, simple-minded, beer-drinking, party-going types, but also as brutal, primitive and vengeful people.

10. Stories told by friends who have been here. Some people base their opinions of south Louisiana partly on stories told by friends who have been here. The logic goes like this: "He's been there, so he ought to know." While these stories may prove to be an accurate reflection of how things really are in south Louisiana, they may also prove to be otherwise. Whether they're true, false or somewhere in between, the firsthand reports of friends can influence a person's thinking about a place.

11. Role-playing on the part of local people. In a gesture of hospitality and cooperation, some south Louisianians are overly anxious to do what the reporters and cameramen want them to do, or to say what they want them to say. So, they'll say things that fit the stereotypes.

For instance, a Louisiana man in the crowd at the LSU-Ohio State football game in Ohio in September of 1988 was eating, and an interviewer asked him if the food was as good as Cajun food.

"Too bland," the Louisiana man said.

"What does it need?" came the leading question from the TV guy.

"More pepper."

Was this man prompted by the interviewer to give that answer? Did he say what he thought the TV man wanted him to say? Or was he simply giving his honest opinion?

An absurd statement that smacks of role-playing was published in the February 1987 issue of *Gentleman's Quarterly*. The writer is Moira Hodgson, and she is quoting one Andy Bergeron, who reportedly taught her how to eat crawfish. Now, if there would be a Most Ridiculous Statements section of the Guinness Book of World Records, this one would have a shot:

"In these parts, if you don't dance and drink beer, people think you're a communist!"

Was this comment unsolicited? Was Mr. Bergeron trying to say something he thought would please the writer, something that would not only comply with the stereotypes but really give her a quotable quote?

There's no doubt in the mind of genealogist Winston DeVille that Cajuns are heavily involved in role-playing for the cameras and the reporters. Much of the responsibility for the image problem with which the Cajun people are burdened can be laid at their own doorsteps, he says.

"The Acadian has abetted the commercialization of his heritage in recent years, as the media have exploited and distorted his lifestyle in a flagrant manner. Never before in history has the Acadian been the focus of so much attention that appeared to be so favorable. Some Acadians have responded much like court jesters . . . ," DeVille says.

12. The high profile of musicians and other entertainers. One reason some people get a false impression of the Cajuns is suggested unwittingly by Thomas Brown in an article in the February 1988 issue of *Continental*, the in-flight magazine of Continental Airlines.

"Cajun musicians (are) the most visible representatives of French Louisiana's culture," he writes, explaining that Cajun bands touring the U.S. and France have enjoyed a high degree of acceptance.

In addition to the bands, much national attention has been drawn to the Cajun culture by Justin Wilson, the humorist and cook. His TV program, "Justin Wilson's Louisiana Cookin'," was voted the most popular cable cooking show in a survey of television viewers in 1988.

While the viewers may like his show, many of the folks back home aren't real excited about the manner in which he represents the Cajun people. Some of the funny stories he tells and the contrived accent in which he tells them are not appreciated by many Cajuns who are proud of their culture and their heritage. They cringe at the thought that other Americans may think Wilson's accent and his mentality are truly reflective of the Cajun people. They are not.

It's true that Cajun musicians and other entertainers are all some people see of this culture, so entertainers are at the forefront of these people's minds when they think of the Cajuns. Take these entertainers and musicians and perhaps something the reader or viewer may have seen about Cajuns being fun-loving and always rockin' and rollin' with the good times, and you've got a firm and fixed, though largely distorted picture of who the Cajuns are.

13. Tourist agencies too limited in their focus. There's no escaping the fact that the state and local tourist agencies have contributed to the stereotyping of the Cajuns and their land. After all, what they advertise and promote constantly are food, music, frolic, swamps and marshes, with a few gardens, museums and mansions thrown in for good measure.

Of course, tourism-promotion agencies cannot be faulted for pushing those things that make their area different and attractive to tourists. It's their job. They must play up the things that are different, the things tourists may never have seen or heard before. To do otherwise, to show what makes south Louisiana like every other part of the country, would certainly spell failure in the highly competitive tourist industry.

But, in the interest of preserving the dignity of the Cajun country and the people who live here, these agencies should make more of an effort to give the travel writers and others counterbalancing information so that the stories don't come out making this area look like a backward part of the nation filled with people whose main purpose in life is to eat, drink and be merry. While a tourist agency representative cannot tell a reporter what to write, his suggestions on what to include and the things he emphasizes can have a substantial influence on the outcome of the story.

14. Proliferation of "Cajun" food products. The flooding of the market with food products labeled "Cajun" may have left the American people with three erroneous impressions. One is that Cajun food is necessarily hot and spicy. Another is that Cajun food can be prepared instantly by sprinkling it with something from a shaker. The third is that because of the sheer number of "Cajun" food products hitting the market, some Americans figure that Cajuns must place disproportional emphasis on the preparation and enjoyment of food.

15. Restaurants serving peppery food and calling it Cajun. It's easy and relatively inexpensive to throw a dish together, sprinkle it with cayenne pepper and call it "Cajun," as has been done by some restaurants in Louisiana and other states. Some people love peppery food and think this is wonderful. Others, who know a good meal when they taste one, think it's terrible; they conclude that if this is Cajun food, they don't want any part of it.

Any of the preceding factors can be responsible for making an impression, either directly or indirectly, upon the observer of the Cajun country, its people, its culture or its food. But when three or four of these factors come into play at once, the impression can be indelible.

For instance, it wouldn't be hard to conclude that Cajun food is peppery hot if you read several national magazines that said it was hot, and you heard this from a friend who had had a hot meal at a restaurant in California, and if, finally, you visited a restaurant in south Louisiana that happened to serve peppery food. With all this, it would be difficult if not impossible for anyone to change your mind — unless perhaps you were invited to enjoy a nice, authentic Cajun meal cooked in one of the homes of south Louisiana.

Another case of several of these factors coming into play at once involves a story that ran in the February 1988 issue of *Continental* magazine. Titled "Some Like It Hot," it was written by Thomas Brown. The writer did a decent job of discussing Cajun history and music then got in over his head by asking:

"What makes a Cajun? What do (these people) have in common?"

Deep question, but shallow answer:

"Ask a Cajun and he might tell you it's *joie de vivre* (joy of life). Everywhere in Cajun country you hear people say, '*Laissez les bon temps rouler*' — Let the good times roll."

Well, in the first place, the reporters write *Laissez les bon temps rouler* a lot more than the local people say it! For some reason, they seem to love that phrase. In the second place, while it may be true that many Cajun people have a number of things in common, it is a gross over-simplification to say only that they share a joy for living, as the writer implies. Moreover, this trait simply does not apply to all Cajuns, and, for that matter, may not even apply to the majority.

It is because of inaccuracies like the one in this article that the reading public forms distorted impressions of the Cajuns. Having gotten a similar impression already from an article in another magazine like *Esquire* and perhaps one from *Town & Country*, and having heard stories that all Cajuns are big party-goers — having thus had this notion reinforced from a variety of sources, how could the reader form any other impression than an erroneous one?

Chapter Eight

Spreading The Truth About The Cajuns

WHAT HAS GONE BEFORE in this book is an effort to portray the Cajuns, their culture and their environment in a realistic manner, to point out that the universe of the average south Louisiana man and woman encompasses a whole lot more than the dining room, the dance hall and the festival grounds.

While the tourism business has boomed in part because of all the publicity this region has received in the 1980s, the publicity has had its down side, as mentioned earlier. The dignity of the Cajuns has been undermined if not assaulted, and some potential new industry has been discouraged from moving here by the image of a workforce which, by many accounts, would seem to be more interested in playing than in working.

The image problem that the Cajuns are faced with is a real one. This image didn't come about overnight, and it's not something that was caused by any one segment of society. It is partly a creation of the Cajuns themselves and partly the doing of the media and the tourism-promotion agencies, among others. While it is a problem that has, to some degree, been around for decades, it is one that has crystalized and intensified in the 1980s as tourism-promotion efforts have increased, reporters and cameramen have flocked in by the hundreds and the commercialization of everything Cajun has reached a fever pitch.

Like any other problem, though, this one has its solutions. A more favorable, more dignified image can be re-built, albeit gradually, if all major parties concerned will recognize their responsibilities in connection with the problem and take the necessary remedial action.

First, the State of Louisiana's tourism-promotion agency, as well as the regional tourist commissions, have a very real responsibility to project a more complete, more dignified image of this region and its people. They can accomplish this goal in part by providing visiting reporters with the kind of counterbalancing information that puts the tourist attractions into a realistic perspective in the overall scheme of things in modern-day Louisiana. This information should not only be provided, but it should be pushed, talked up, as a means of increasing the chances that it will be included in the feature articles.

This is not to suggest that these agencies should cut back on the promotion of south Louisiana's intriguing tourist attractions. On the contrary, the State, especially, should increase its advertising budget, considering the tremendously favorable return on the money it has invested in tourism advertising.

But it is to suggest that in addition to their basic work of promoting the tourist attractions, they could develop fact sheets or media packets containing the previously mentioned counterbalancing information and have this material as readily available to reporters as the tourist brochures. They could also develop programs to train people working in the tourism business, both public and private, to talk more knowledgeably with visitors not only about the tourist attractions but also about the other positive aspects of their state.

Secondly, the Cajuns and others living in Acadiana can help to correct the image problem by conducting themselves in a manner befitting a people with a proud heritage. It can be done, in part, by not reciting to reporters and visitors the tired, old lines that depict Cajuns and their neighbors as less enlightened than other Americans. It can be done by avoiding role-playing, particularly the role that casts the Cajun as the simple-minded, fun-loving type that some of the tourists and media people have come to expect.

This isn't to suggest that most Cajuns and their neighbors play this role, because such is not the case. It is to point out, though, that too many do, and that it would surely help the cause if they didn't.

Thirdly, writers, editors, photographers and producers can help remedy this image problem by allowing more time and making more of an effort when they do feature stories on the Cajuns and the Cajun country. In the bargain, they'll come up with better-balanced, less-stereotyping stories.

Journalists' primary responsibility is to their readers or viewers, to deliver factual, balanced, meaningful information to the reading or viewing public. They also have an important second responsibility, and that is to the subjects about whom they are writing, to be fair and balanced in what they report. Both of these responsibilities are better served when the information-gathering is more thorough and the writing more accurate — when the facts about south Louisiana's tourist attractions are put into a more balanced perspective, for instance.

To achieve this perspective, they need to broaden the base of who they interview. Instead of talking with only three or four people who are in the tourism business, they could also interview three or four who aren't. They could interview the people who operate the Center for Louisiana Studies on the USL campus, or the professors who are knowledgeable in Acadian culture on the staff of Nicholls State University in Thibodaux. They could talk with people who have lived here all their lives, such as men and women who own the auto dealerships and the retail stores or who operate the financial institutions, the hardware stores or the sugarcane farms.

The use of a wider range of sources would help generate superior stories — stories that would come closer to the truth about the Cajuns.

— The End —

About the Author

TRENT ANGERS is editor and publisher of *Acadiana Profile*, "The Magazine of the Cajun Country," based in Lafayette, La. He has worked with the magazine since 1970, first as a reporter and photographer and later taking over as editor and publisher, in 1977. The magazine, founded in 1968 by his parents, Geraldine and the late Robert Angers, is the longest-living independent magazine in Louisiana history.

Angers graduated from Louisiana State University in 1970 and was named the Outstanding Graduating Senior in Journalism by Sigma Delta Chi, professional journalism organization. He also won the Hodding Carter Award for Responsible Journalism. While attending LSU he served a term as news editor and then managing editor of *The Daily Reveille*, the college newspaper, and an apprenticeship at the *Palm Beach Post*.

In the early 1970s he was a staff correspondent for the *New Orleans Times-Picayune* and the *Beaumont Enterprise*, and he wrote free-lance stories for a dozen other south Louisiana newspapers. His career in journalism began at age 14 on the newspaper his father owned, the *Banner-Tribune*, in Franklin, La., where he was first a photographer, then a reporter.

A student of Louisiana history and the history of the Cajun people, Angers was born in 1948 in New Iberia, La., in the heart of the Cajun country, and he has lived in this area all his life.

Want to know more about the Cajuns and their culture?

Much of what you may want to know about the Cajuns, their land, their history and culture can be found in the pages of *Acadiana Profile*, "The Magazine of the Cajun Country," and in its special issues, cookbooks, tour guide and other fine products. For example:

- "Louisiana's French Heritage"
- "The Origin of South Louisiana Family Names"
- "In Search of a Friendly Land"
- Cajun Country Tour Guide
- Guide to the Fairs & Festivals of Cajun Country
- "The Character of the Cajun Country" (A Pictorial)
- "Cajun Cooking" Cookbook (A set of two)

For a free brochure, write to Acadiana Profile, P.O. Box 52247, Lafayette, La. 70505.

(Additional copies of "The Truth About The Cajuns" can also be ordered through Acadiana Profile.)